THE ANGER WORKBOOK

Lorrainne Bilodeau, M.S.

HAZELDEN®

INFORMATION & EDUCATIONAL SERVICES

Hazelden
Center City, Minnesota 55012-1076

ISBN: 1-56838-054-2

To Mike and Elaine, two friends who were the victims of anger gone awry.

CONTENTS

This guide is not meant to supplant professional counseling or therapy. If you have destructive thoughts about yourself or someone else, seek professional advice.

Author's Note

The other evening I was sitting with some friends when the topic turned to self-help books. As I expounded rather negatively on the subject, I noticed that my friends were staring at me with puzzled, curious looks on their faces. The light bulb went on, and I blurted out, "God forgive me! I have written a self-help book."

Well, that's the truth—although I do need to warn you: it is an **informational manual.** You will not find soothing phrases that seem immediately to elevate your mood. You won't find easy answers. And you won't find a whole new you. You will find serious information that explains anger and its uses. You will find a new perspective that, along with a great deal of effort and honesty in working the exercises, will help you change the way you experience and use anger.

There are many people I would like to blame for this overwhelming endeavor. Instead I will do the polite, socially acceptable thing and say thanks to the following:

Ray Matheson, who in 1982 asked me to do a workshop for professionals entitled, "Working with the Angry Client." It was the first time I had to present my ideas about anger in an orderly, understandable fashion. I never suspected what would emerge from that first workshop.

Ed Kavanaugh, Mindy Burgin-Debyshire, and Phyllis T. McCafferty, who all took a risk to facilitate the "Encountering Anger" Clinic, which put the theories of this manual to use.

Dan Scott, Susie Sheppard, Eric Van Quill, and Mary Netsley (the counselors at Richmond Aftercare), who not only put up with me, but supported and laughed with me through my periods of anxiety, elation, and irritability.

Ruthy Kossove, who went out of her way to supply an essential piece of reference material.

And special thanks to Carole Sutton, who said, "Write a manual. It's easier than a book." (I really think it's the last time she'll utter those words.) Her kindness, encouragement, and laughter kept me going.

CHAPTER ONE

Investigating Personal Attitudes about Anger

Recently a colleague observed that, if the world is destroyed, the cataclysm will happen because intellectual growth has far outpaced humankind's emotional development. People's inability to curb, or at least control their emotions will lead to gross abuse of technology. When I asked whether my colleague meant all feelings or just anger, he thought a moment and responded, "Most feelings, but especially anger."

In a way I agree with him. It is emotional immaturity that incites destructive behavior. But I must take exception to his solution, the curbing or controlling of emotions. This very approach to human feelings has caused the problem. People make decisions and act on feelings that they don't even know they have. This kind of behavior is not emotional maturity, but its opposite. Emotionally mature people recognize, understand, and use emotions in their intended functions.

As long as we believe, like my colleague, that feelings must be stopped, controlled, or avoided, we misspend our energies. Attempts to stamp out feelings inevitably lead to failure. No matter what methods a person tries, feelings aren't stopped—they continue to occur. They aren't avoided—they remain hidden. And because they are hidden, beyond our awareness, they control us. This process leads some people to a very hurtful emotional trap. Their feelings have been hidden away for so long that, when they realize they need them and try to access them, they can't.

I counseled a couple who were trying to cope with the discovery that their child was severely learning disabled. They had sought counseling because the wife, Janet, had begun avoiding all three of her children. During one session, the husband, Roy, with desperation showing in every feature, looked at his wife and said in the gentlest voice, "I need to know how you feel about this. Are you angry or what?" We sat in silence as Janet looked down at her hands, then at me, and finally back to Roy. Her voice held a tone of failure as she replied, "I wish I could tell you, but I just don't know."

Over time and with hard work, Janet discovered that she had many feelings about her child's disability. She felt guilty, thinking it was somehow her fault. She felt afraid that she wouldn't be able to provide the parenting necessary to help her daughter. She felt sad when she thought about the obstacles her daughter would have to overcome. She felt angry that God had given her a burden that other parents didn't have to bear.

As with so many people, anger was the most difficult emotion for her to recognize, openly discuss, and use productively. She had many years of misunderstanding and misinformation to overcome. The idea that anger was bad, dangerous, and unladylike was deeply ingrained by her parents and supported by others as she went through life. Janet had become so adept at denying her anger that she believed what others said about her, that she was a "nice" person who never got angry. Then an event happened that triggered an anger so intense that it forced her to behave in ways that were contrary to her nature.

I read about Janet in the local paper five years after she had left counseling. She was spearheading a project to provide special programs funded by the city for learning disabled children. I couldn't resist calling to ask what had brought her to that point. She said, "Lorrainne, I was afraid my daughter wouldn't get what she needed and it pissed me off. So I got off my duff and did something about it." Janet had reached emotional maturity. She recognized her anger, understood that it could be used as a motivator, and took constructive action to bring about positive change.

Whether you have difficulty with anger because you can't feel it or because it seems to overwhelm you, the path to change begins with one simple truth: Anger is a common, normal emotion.

For me, a simple errand at the grocery store presents myriad situations that may result in a range of angry feelings. For instance, I feel some level of anger when someone pulls into a parking space that I was aiming for; the grocery cart I choose has a defective wheel; people block the aisle with their carts, and they're nowhere in sight; I carefully pick only nine items (foregoing my favorite snack to make the nine) so I can use the express lane, and the woman in front of me has twelve items and pays by check; the store uses only tiny plastic bags that hold five items, instead of paper bags with three times that capacity; or I return to my car, and someone has rammed a cart into it.

I could go on and on with more examples of the times I've felt some kind of anger, from mild annoyance to intense fury, while performing tasks as simple as buying the basic necessities of life at a grocery store. There's no need. The few examples I've offered make my point: anger occurs every day, many times a day.

Denial of this common emotion is the result of misinformation received as truth. This misinformation then becomes the foundation for strongly entrenched attitudes about anger that result in its misuse. Changing attitudes and developing new behaviors involve hard work and effort. Entrenched and deeply hidden attitudes must be brought to light, knowledge and understanding gained, new ways of responding developed and practiced. At times the task seems too difficult and tiring. As I have made mistakes and struggled with this process myself, I have often asked if it is worth it. Then something happens, and I have the freedom to feel and use my emotion, instead of being used by it, and my answer becomes a resounding yes—the effort was worth it.

The work begins with discovering the attitudes you have about anger that may inhibit your ability to recognize and use it. That process is the purpose of the following exercises. As you complete them, be honest. Don't worry about getting the "right" answer. The right answer is *your* answer. You will use that response later in the book to understand where your anger has gone awry and to develop new information, approaches, and responses to anger that are right for you.

Don't limit yourself to the space provided on these pages. A notebook may be helpful for doing the exercises more completely and for writing down ideas as they occur when you read the informational chapters.

What Makes You Angry?

Everyone experiences anger—some people more intensely than others; some more frequently. Everyone I have asked has been able to come up with something that incites anger. Here are some of the most common answers that I've heard to the question, "What makes you angry?" Which ones are true for you? Are there some you'd like to add?

☐	Traffic jams	☐	Inconsiderate people
☐	Arrogance	☐	Injustice
☐	Rude people	☐	Taxes
☐	Prejudice	☐	People who cheat me
☐	Tailgaters	☐	People who cut in line
☐	Yelling	☐	Disbelief of what I say
☐	Manipulation of my time	☐	Workers who don't do their jobs
☐	Tardiness	☐	My paycheck
☐	Child abuse	☐	Criticism
☐	Waiting	☐	People who won't listen
☐	Lies	☐	False accusations
☐	_____	☐	_____
☐	_____	☐	_____
☐	_____	☐	_____
☐	_____	☐	_____
☐	_____	☐	_____
☐	_____	☐	_____
☐	_____	☐	_____
☐	_____	☐	_____
☐	_____	☐	_____
☐	_____	☐	_____
☐	_____	☐	_____

How Would You Describe Anger?

Everyone has ideas about what anger is and what it looks like. Recognition of anger occurs when its appearance matches one of these ideas. Listed below are words that people have told me describe anger. Which do you agree with? Are there any you'd like to add?

☐ Redness	☐ Simmering	☐ Cursing
☐ Loudness	☐ Tension	☐ Put-downs
☐ Volcano	☐ Destruction	☐ Silence
☐ Heat	☐ Yelling	☐ Withholding
☐ Sarcasm	☐ Tears	☐ Verbal abuse
☐ Hitting	☐ Control	☐ Violence

The ability to recognize anger is initially learned by children who watch how angry adults act. The observed behaviors become cues for future adult recognition of anger. Remembering your childhood, how would you describe the anger demonstrated by the adults you lived with?

_____

_____

_____

_____

_____

_____

_____

_____

_____

_____

What Are Your Expectations?

Children learn to fear anger when the behaviors demonstrated by angry adults result in physical or emotional pain. They learn that something unpleasant follows when someone is angry. This conditioning continues throughout life, and the expectation of this unpleasantness occurs every time someone is angry.

When you were a child, what happened to you when others were angry?

_____

What did you think? _____

_____

What did you feel? _____

_____

How Did You Respond?

A person's basic style of response to another's anger develops during childhood. This style modifies and expands with day-to-day experience in handling situations encountered as an adult. The basic style remains. As a child, when an adult's anger was directed toward you,

What did you think? _____

_____

What did you feel? _____

_____

What did you do? _____

_____

How did you evaluate yourself afterwards? _____

_____

How Do You Respond to Anger?

People react to anger in others. This reaction produces a behavioral response. Both reaction and response were learned during childhood. As individuals grow older, they develop adult versions of this early style.

How do you respond to other people's anger now?_____

_____ _____

What are your internal reactions (thoughts and feelings)?   _____

_____

What is your external response (actions)?   _____

_____

What Is Your Fantasy Response?

After you have been involved in an angry episode in which someone else acted out anger, what is your fantasy of what you said or did?

_____

_____

What Is the Ideal Response?

In your mind, what is an ideal, healthy response to another's anger?

_____

_____

_____

_____

_____

What Your Answers Show about Attitudes

Now that you have completed the exercises, you have focused energy and spent time on your experiences with angry feelings. You have looked from many directions at your own anger and your responses to other people's anger. Your answers are meaningful indicators of your fundamental assumptions. You may be thinking, "I already know what my attitudes are about anger." As you read on, however, you may be surprised to discover a difference between what you think your attitudes are and what your answers suggest. More often than not, our strongest attitudes are those most deeply hidden. This defense occurs even in highly trained counselors who claim that they believe anger to be a positive, normal emotion. After studying their answers to the exercises, "How Would You Describe Anger?" and "What Is the Ideal Response?," many therapist realize that their underlying attitudes about angry feelings are very negative.

Because these hidden attitudes show themselves in behaviors, they exert a powerful influence over interactions with others. Therefore, it is important to bring them to light. Only then can steps be taken to minimize their control.

What Makes You Angry?

If you agreed with the entire list, "What Makes You Angry?," you're in the company of many hundreds of people who helped construct the list.

Maybe you're a person who has said, "I never get angry. It's a waste of energy. It doesn't change anything, so why bother?" If so, what you are saying is that there has never been anything or anyone (yourself included) important enough to protect, defend, or fight for. I don't think that's true. More likely, you have felt angry and didn't realize it.

If you didn't agree that prejudice, child abuse, and injustice make you angry, and if you don't take offense when people cheat you or ignore you, then there is a good chance that you believe anger is bad or dangerous or hurtful. This belief is so strong and its resultant fear so great that your anger remains hidden, even from yourself. For it is at these times when anger is not only okay but necessary for your well-being or the well-being of someone else.

How Would You Describe Anger?

Most, if not all, of the descriptive words from this exercise are negative in tone. They connote a danger that is either overt or just below the very thin layer of human control. They suggest that anger is injurious, harmful, and painfully potent.

If you agreed with all or any of the descriptive words in the list, then you see anger as unpleasant and hurtful. On some level, you fear anger. Even if you added to the list some positive, descriptive words—such as "energizing," "motivating," or "constructive"—those words would be minimal compared to the number of negative words.

Many people say that they don't think anger is bad, but upon closer examination, their behavior indicates otherwise. I encountered a vivid example of this when I was interviewed for a local newspaper. For over an hour the reporter and I talked about the virtues of anger. She nodded and verbally agreed with what I said throughout the interview. I told about an angry incident from my life to illustrate a point. When the article was written, the reporter stated, "Even Ms. Bilodeau is not immune from anger." It was clear to me that, although the reporter may agree on an intellectual level that anger is okay, somewhere deeper within she believes anger is bad. "Immune" means "protected from a disease" or "exempt." The reporter's words gave away her underlying attitude about anger. If anger is good, why would I want "immunity" from it?

When looked at together, the first two exercises, "What Makes You Angry?" and "How Would You Describe Anger?", explain the human conflict engendered by anger. On the one side is the reality that anger is so common that people normally feel it many times every day. On the other side are deeply entrenched attitudes that say angry feelings are bad, hurtful, and dangerous. A person is continuously required to experience a feeling he deems harmful to his well-being.

In resolving this conflict, people most often find themselves doing one of three things:

- **Never feeling anger.** A highly-developed defense system does not allow anger to emerge. It remains hidden until an experience is so powerful that the anger bursts out.

- **Feeling anger and not expressing it.** When the anger asserts itself, it is usually misdirected or excessive for the situation.

- **Feeling anger and expressing it in an aggressive, hurtful way.**

Each of these responses hurts the self or others and therefore compounds the conflict by reaffirming the belief that anger is bad, dangerous, or hurtful.

What Are Your Expectations?

This exercise shows how much power is given to anger in an individual's life.

If a youngster witnesses explosive, destructive, angry behavior at home, then he comes to expect that everyone's anger is violent. An angry incident means someone or something is going to be hurt. Verbally abusive episodes encountered as a child result in the expectation that, when anger occurs, someone will be put down and emotionally brutalized. If anger is expressed with cold silence or harsh glares, or pointed indifference, a child hears the powerful message, "You're not important; I don't love you. You don't exist. You're not worthy of a response." This silent treatment is abusive, for it damages a person's self-esteem.

If you have experienced any of these skewed behaviors, then you have been taught that anger is dangerous, and the bearer of angry feelings is bad. The frequency, intensity, and duration of painful anger episodes in your childhood determine the amount of power you bestow on anger, the level of fear you have about it, and the harshness with which you judge the person who is angry, yourself or another.

If your parents didn't allow you to see their expressions of anger, your ideas about this emotion are probably confused. Their behavior was a strong statement that angry feelings don't exist in adults. You grew up with no model for understanding your own anger. You had no label for it. You had no way of knowing how to express it or respond to it. If you believed that your parents didn't feel anger, you might have wondered what is wrong with those who do. In fact, as an adult you may still find anger confusing.

How Did You Respond? How Do You Respond?

These two exercises help illustrate the fact that people's problems with anger occur because they are adults coping from a child's perspective. In other words, they try to respond to adult situations from a child's position of vulnerability and powerlessness. Children depend upon adults for the basic necessities of life, for food, shelter, love, acceptance, approval, and self-identity. When these adults act out their angry feelings in hurtful ways, children see their necessities threatened. Survival is at stake. The danger is immediate; the fear intense.

Did you believe the anger was your fault? Did you respond by trying harder to do right? To be perfect? Or did you rebel and fight back? Did you hide in order to avoid angry scenes? Did you see the world as a place where you didn't belong? Did you evaluate yourself as bad, stupid, or not "good enough"?

As an adult, if you look closely, you will find the same pattern. For instance, if your response as a child was to try harder, now when your boss expresses anger because of a mistake, you probably put forth more effort to make sure it doesn't happen again. If the error was that of someone else, you either help that person or act for him next time. Your motivator is to do the job right in order to avoid anger. If you withdrew as a child, you have probably learned to withdraw mentally as an adult. You may still seek physical isolation when possible. Situations from which you cannot physically escape, you know how to escape in your mind. Even in a crowd of people, you are alone. And if you fought back as a child, you probably do the same now. You may even find yourself fighting other people's battles. This response might be seen as a social attribute, except that you have learned to fight in an aggressively destructive manner.

If you have been responding to anger in any of these ways for twenty, thirty, or forty years, you may have discovered that they are ineffective and costly. No matter how perfect you become, others are still angry. The cost, your self-esteem. You are never "good enough." The perfect housewife finds that her husband nevertheless feels angry. No matter how aggressive you are in fighting, you lose because people with more authority beat you. When you beat others with less authority, acting like the boss who berates his workers, for example, everyone sees *you* as the abuser, the bully. The cost, your self-esteem. Either way, you lose. No matter how hard you try, the only way to hide from anger is to withdraw totally from the world. The cost, your humanity. And that's a high price to pay because we are social creatures who need interaction with others.

What Is Your Fantasy Response?

Normally, after an angry exchange in which there is no resolution, a person mentally relives the incident in solitude. During this process the scene is embellished with ideas of what could have been done, should have been done, or might be done next time.

Did your fantasy involve violence? The violence could be physical, such as striking or maiming; it could be emotional, such as clever put-downs, sarcasm, or telling the person off. Somehow, in your recreated scenario, you struck back at the angry individual. If so, you may believe anger to be a form of power, a weapon. Seeing anger as an attack on you, you counterattack. An angry incident becomes a power struggle. In your fantasy, you may use anger to come out on top.

Perhaps you see another person's anger as disapproval, a statement that you are wrong. Your embellished script allows you the last word, the winning blow. You're not wrong; the other person is. Or perhaps you permit yourself anger only when you're in the right. Anger takes on a right vs. wrong quality. It's a judgment.

Did your fantasy involve placating the angry person? Somehow getting him to stop being angry? Did you envision yourself storming out of the room, slamming the door as you left? If so, you may see anger as a device of punishment, a potentially hazardous weapon that produces physical harm or emotional destruction. You want to stop it before it occurs, or get out of its way to avoid harm.

In your fantasy did you put yourself down? Perhaps you thought, "I'm wrong. I'm no good. I shouldn't have made him angry. It's my fault. I'll never do this right." If so, you may believe that a person's anger is controlled by external forces. You also seem to view anger as an evaluation of self. Again, anger has become a means of disapproval, of judgment.

What Is the Ideal Response?

People who answer this question in my workshops most commonly propose these responses: leave the room; remove yourself until the angry person becomes rational; stay calm and maintain control; and let the person ventilate. Although these choices seem reasonable, consider the implications. Feeling that you must leave an angry person suggests an attitude that anger is dangerous. Humans run from things they fear, things they think will be painful, hurtful, or fatal.

The idea of removing yourself until the person is rational stems from the belief that anger either comes from or creates irrationality. Anger equals insanity.

If you must remain calm and maintain control, what are you controlling? Yourself? The other person? The situation? What terrible thing happens if you don't stay calm and in control?

If you suggest allowing the angry person to ventilate, you present a vivid picture of anger as steam in a pressure cooker. It is hot, pressurized, and explosive. If a valve isn't turned to let some steam escape, a catastrophe will occur.

This whole idea of ventilation stems from the theory that people stockpile anger in a reservoir. When the reservoir gets too full, it spills over in the form of an aggressive incident. Letting the anger out lowers the reservoir, and avoids an aggressive episode. If you have ever known a person who is often explosive with his anger, you can understand the illogic of this whole theory. The reservoir should be lowered with each explosion. If the person explodes often enough, the reservoir should run dry, yet he keeps exploding. In fact, if you look closely, you discover that, with time, these incidents increase.

Misinformation about anger is often presented in subtle, behavioral ways, without anyone's stopping to realize what is being taught. I was at a friend's house when her daughter began acting out. My friend's husband asked the girl to go upstairs and watch TV. She ignored her father and continued to be loud and disruptive. Finally, he took her by the shoulders, looked her directly in the eye, and in a menacing voice said, "Daddy's getting angry." The child turned and went upstairs.

The immediate result seemed to be success—for the father. Unfortunately for the child, anger has become a threat. Something bad happens when someone is angry. She has also been taught that she is responsible for other people's anger. Are these lessons true? She won't even consider the question because, to her, they are a reality. And her reality will be validated many times over by her father and other adults who blame and threaten her when angry. She will continue to believe in this reality and act accordingly throughout her life unless something intervenes which forces her to question its validity. Even then, she will probably find it difficult to judge false what seemed real for so long.

You may find yourself in that position now because the lessons you have learned about anger are pervasive and deeply entrenched. We all are taught these lessons at a young age; we learn them experientially, and they are continually validated throughout our lives by others who had learned the same lessons. Consequently, you may never have thought to question the accuracy of the information.

While doing the exercises and reading the commentary, perhaps you discovered that you hold many of the ideas and attitudes described in this chapter. You may be ready to argue that these attitudes are what anger is all about, that the beliefs you've maintained for many years are right. They have brought you this far. They may be right for you.

For the time being, don't worry about right or wrong. Instead, consider whether you are satisfied with the way you handle anger—your own and others'. Does your anger make you more effective as a human being? Do you feel okay with yourself after an angry episode? If not, then some changes are in order. And the place to start is by informing yourself about anger so that you can view it from a different, less frightening perspective.

CHAPTER TWO

Taking a New Perspective on Anger

As I go through each day, tending to the daily duties and pleasures of life, I encounter many different people doing the same. I watch them and talk with them and feel sad. So many of these people deny the aspect of themselves that makes them most fully human—the ability to have and enjoy emotions: to feel about, to feel toward, to feel for.

I have a friend who once argued that "negative" feelings couldn't be enjoyable. I reminded her that she'd seen five showings of the movie *Love Story* and cried each time. If sadness is so unenjoyable, why pay money, not once but five times, to live through a sad experience? The same is true of fear. Whenever a new ride, supposedly more scary than the last, is built at the amusement park, she makes it a point to be one of the first to ride it. If fear is so bad, why pay to be frightened? Anyone's average day can provide the same emotions for free.

There is a difference. At the movies or amusement parks people let themselves experience these feelings without judging them bad or unacceptable. The misinformation about feelings that operates during most of the day, people set aside during such activities. They stop fighting the emotion and allow themselves to experience it for just what it is and nothing more. The result can actually be a pleasant sensation. The emotion itself isn't what is most unpleasant; the judgments about it cause the greatest discomfort.

Only by moving beyond these judgments and the resultant discomfort can a person learn to experience emotions, including anger, as they occur. Anyone who understands what anger really is can set aside misconceptions and realize that, like any emotion, it is functional. Not only is anger not dangerous; it can be useful.

Anger Is a Feeling

Most people agree that anger is a feeling, an emotion. With only a quick glance and not much thought, this view appears to be a simple, clear-cut idea. But what do the words "emotion" and "feeling" mean? We must agree on a workable, practical understanding of the vocabulary.

An emotion or feeling is an *internal reaction*. This reaction is a biophysiological response, a physical sensation, created when certain chemicals increase in the body.[1] When the body releases endorphins, for instance, a sensation of contentment and well-being results. Humans recognize this physical reaction as happiness or gladness.

The "re-" in reaction indicates that the chemicals and the resultant sensation are a response *to* something, usually *to an external event* or stimulation. Feelings may occur without an external stimulus when a biophysiological, chemical imbalance is present. This imbalance can be as minor as that caused by hunger, which produces an anxious feeling, or as major as the imbalance that causes manic-depression, an illness with vast mood swings. When the imbalance is corrected, the feelings fade. Some people may argue that no external event has occurred when they imagine or create an incident in their minds and then experience emotional responses to these mental images. In this situation, the event is similar to the images of a movie, but this "movie" is viewed on a screen in a very private projection room. The mind suspends reality, and the person experiences the scenes as though they were really happening in the present. In essence, part of the mind operates on the belief that the "show" is a real-life, external event.

Defining an emotion as an internal reaction to an external event is adequate only in the discussion of animals other than man. At this level, feelings are instinctive and used most often for physical survival. Human beings still have this primitive aspect in their array of functioning abilities. It comes from what can be called the "old brain" and is experienced most intensely during times of immediate danger, when survival depends on action without thought.

Through evolution, the human mind has developed what can be considered an additional brain. This "new brain," the neocortex, provides the human species with the unique faculty to abstract, symbolize, and convey information. With this development, we gained the ability to think about, differentiate, and label various internal reactions. Since the new brain is not an organ that operates on instinct, we must learn these functions. With this learning, emotions take on another dimension which must be included in the definition: socialization.

A human being learns to name her internal reactions. This labeling involves experiencing, differentiating, and naming each biophysiological sensation. People learn this complex behavior at a young age. In one study, children knew how to label the four basic emotions with the descriptive words of mad, glad, sad, and afraid, by the age of six.[2] If such young children have learned, they must have had teachers, the people immediately involved in children's lives.

This understanding of an emotion or feeling permits a definition of anger:

> *Anger is an internal reaction,*
> *which an individual learns to name,*
> *to an external event.*

The emotional process is straightforward and physically based. An incident occurs that stimulates the brain to direct the production of the chemical necessary for an anger response. The physical sensation consists of increased heart and pulse rate, shallow, quick breathing, flushed skin, increased muscle tension, increased temperature, and possible tremors and perspiration. These biophysiological reactions happen because an extra supply of a stimulant has been added to the blood stream. The metabolism speeds up and the body responds accordingly. The individual labels the complete experience "anger."

From this perspective, anger certainly doesn't seem so inauspicious. In fact, when I saw my friend's husband look at their child and say in a menacing voice, "Daddy's getting angry," I very much wanted to respond, "What's the big deal? Daddy has a little extra adrenaline and the ability to label it." But I refrained. I thought it wouldn't help the father's attitude or the child's situation.

The important point is that anger, like any other emotion, is nothing more than the body's internal response to the release of a natural chemical. It removes much of the emotion's potency to realize that, in itself, anger isn't dangerous, threatening, or hurtful.

Anger Is Not a Gigantic Mistake

Every emotion has a result directly related to the well-being of humanity. Loneliness brings people together, forming social units, and through numbers and cooperation, making it possible for the species not only to survive, but to dominate the world. Guilt helps to keep order and to restrain behavior by indicating violations of socially dictated values. Fear signals danger. It is the body's warning that a threatening situation is at hand. It alerts a person to readiness.

Anger is no exception, nor was it a colossal mistake, in the development of *Homo sapiens*. Evolution did not take a wrong turn, and through some bizarre quirk of nature, produce a mutation of brain or gene which resulted in an unnatural, deviant emotion that reduced the chances for further development and species enrichment.

In fact, anger has many functions. Modern life would be very different and much more difficult if anger had been omitted or eliminated from the human experience.

Survival

Of anger's many functions the most basic is survival. Without it, the human race probably wouldn't have made it to this century—or, if it had, far fewer people would be alive today.

Anger is a necessary ingredient in hands-on fighting. Although that factor may not seem important in modern civilization, it was crucial before the technological era when physical defense against larger, stronger animals demanded that a human fight or be killed.

Anger is the emotion that provided the incentive to struggle against the elements and to accomplish what would have been physically impossible without the additional strength that seems to accompany anger. Adrenaline, the chemical involved in anger arousal, produces a numbing effect on the body which allows a person to continue fighting when hurt. The individual doesn't experience pain until after the struggle, when the adrenaline level drops.

This dampening of pain serves another purpose: it makes the human being stronger. The body's strength is far greater in anger than in average activities. If exertion is attempted when adrenaline is not present, pain limits what the body can do. Without pain, the body comes closer to reaching its absolute strength potential. This power makes the human being's success in a physical struggle more likely. Anger also creates a tunnel-vision effect that concentrates attention onto the opposing force. During the struggle, the individual's energies cannot be diverted easily. Anger allows him to focus on the battle. Both external and internal distractions are eliminated. Self-doubt and fear of failure do not impinge on the combatant's ability to struggle. In effect, the individual does not defeat the self.

Culture

Anger functions in any culture as a social regulator. It defines social behavior and protects societal values. Each culture determines when an angry response is appropriate and how that response is to be expressed. Anger is considered appropriate when the norms, mores, and laws of the culture are violated. The intensity of the response depends upon the importance of the violations. Thus anger defines the boundaries of acceptable behavior for social situations. What I considered a rather innocuous behavior, a woman's hugging Queen Elizabeth during a visit to America, received media coverage around the world. An English friend of mine was outraged, exclaiming, "How dare she touch the Queen!" I thought, Why not? A good hug never hurt anybody. To my friend's way of thinking, formed by her English upbringing, the norms established for royalty had been violated, and she responded with anger.

This function of anger can be seen in the list, "What Makes You Angry?" The answers—rude people, prejudice, yelling, child abuse, and inconsiderate people—are all culturally determined. Each society sets the definition of rudeness, inconsideration, and child abuse. While disciplining a child, for instance, a Native American might find it rude and become angry if the child looked at him. An Irish American might become angry if the child *didn't* look at him. Culture determines what is deemed inconsiderate.

The "generation gap" is also a culture gap. Child abuse in America has been defined differently from one generation to another. "Spare the rod, spoil the child" was a guiding rule of child-rearing during my parents' youth. Many people my age, however, become angry when they witness parents controlling children's behavior by using any type of physical punishment.

Perceptions of rudeness also differ in various regions because of culture. A person from the Bronx may hear patrons in a genteel southern restaurant mutter, "How rude," if he yells out his order. In his natural environment, a New York deli during lunch hour, this behavior won't be noticed; in fact, it may be the only way he can get lunch.

Anger also functions as a *social bond.* When a group of people focuses anger collectively on an outside group, individual, or situation, the shared anger ties individuals of the group together. They have a common enemy. The lines of "we vs. they" are drawn.[3] To be a member of the "we" group, an individual must be angry at the "they" group. This phenomenon is often observable in the workplace, where persons of diverse personal interests come together for eight hours a day, their common bond being the way they earn a living.

Coworkers may build cohesiveness by developing angry feelings focused on a mutual enemy. Their conversation may ridicule outsiders with sarcasm or gossip. This enemy can be the management, another unit, an individual not in the group, or another company. To belong in the group, an individual must take an active role in these conversations because it is this behavior that fuels the anger, draws the involved people together, and strengthens the sense of "we." A person who does not participate in the angry discussions is not considered a part of the group. In fact, when not physically present in the group, she may even become a "they."

This bonding may undermine worker morale and, at times, may hamper job performance or even result in sabotage, especially when cooperation between units, management, other companies, and diverse workers is essential to production. If performance is contingent on competition with outsiders, the anger produced by this type of social bonding can be used as an incentive for greater effort and harder work. In the 1991 World Series, for example, managers put columns from the opposing city's newspapers on bulletin boards to stir the home team.

Another highly visible form of social bonding by anger occurs in activist groups. Often these groups comprise people from very different walks of life, who have little in common except angry feelings about a particular social issue. When the social issue is resolved, the group either disbands or focuses on another issue. Some group members may not share the same anger about the new issue and therefore drop out of the group. New members may join who do not feel angry about the first issue but do about the second. It isn't the issues, but the angry feelings *about* the issues that bring and hold the individuals together as a group.

Activist groups demonstrate another cultural function of anger. Angry feelings act as the ignition and impetus for *social change.* Without anger over social injustice, America would still be under British rule and paying taxes to England; Afro-Americans would still be enslaved; and women would still be the property of their husbands. In each of these situations and countless others, it was anger about a social injustice that provided people with the motivation and necessary courage to stand up against a strongly entrenched system and, at the risk of their own well-being, fight for change. Without anger, these battles would never have been started. If started, they certainly would never have been sustained.

Communication

Anger is a vehicle of communication that always carries a message. The person who expresses anger is trying to present information. Often it is information that, without the anger, he wouldn't have the courage to express. The importance placed on the message by the sender determines the intensity of anger presented. The reverse is also true; the greater the anger, the more valuable the communication is to the sender. If the intended receiver doesn't indicate that the information has been heard, the sender often emphasizes the message with stronger signals of anger, reinforcing the importance of the communication. If you have ever watched a child ignore a parental directive, you know exactly what I'm talking about. When the directive is repeated, you can hear the parent's voice become louder and the tone angrier.

Describing anger, many people use the word "violent." Psychiatrist Albert Rothenberg contends, however, that, used as a tool of communication, anger actually *reduces* episodes of violent behavior. Instead of resorting to violence when faced with a threatening or obstructive situation, "the angry individual can employ verbal discharge and a whole series of specific communications to others designed to promote removal of the threat or obstruction."[4] As the first response to a threatening or frustrating situation, verbally communicated anger reduces the use of physical attack. If an angry tone of voice or facial expression or command defuses the situation, then the necessity for violence diminishes.

Motivation

When a person uses anger constructively, it acts as a motivating force for change, for meeting personal needs, and for gaining a desired goal.

In 1982, I was sitting in my office, angry about an incident with my supervisor. Mentally I was calling her every nasty name that I had heard throughout my life. Finally, the question occurred to me, "Why is she the supervisor, when I'm better at this work than she?" I looked over at her office wall. She had a master's degree, and I didn't. As long as I didn't, people like her would supervise me and dictate my work life.

At that moment, I had a variety of choices. I could wallow in the injustice of the system, making myself a victim and sloshing around in self-pity for the rest of my career. I could become aggressive, bound into her office, tell her everything she was doing wrong, and say that the only reason she was the supervisor was that she had a piece of paper. Or, I could direct my anger toward the goal of obtaining a master's degree myself. Two days later I was enrolled in college again and had submitted a request for a leave of absence. Anger's usefulness didn't end there. Whenever I had to work late on an exam, a paper, or my finals and felt myself being overtaken by drowsiness, I pictured that woman in my mind. My adrenaline started to flow. I was good for another hour's work.

In many situations, anger needs to be experienced and properly channeled before positive action can be taken. These circumstances are often accompanied by the thoughts, "That's it. I've had enough. I deserve better." Battered women present a good example of what I've been talking about. One reason some women can't get out of a battering relationship is that, when they are able to feel their anger, they are unable to channel it toward a productive goal. They discover that their ill-used anger only leads to more battering. For survival, they hide their angry feelings until the day comes when they cross an invisible line and no longer can feel their anger or anything else. Others, hearing a battered woman's story, think she must be irate, yet she seems to feel nothing. With badly bruised self-esteem and a history of suffering anger's violent potential, battered women have learned to flee this emotion. Without help, they cannot experience the anger that they need to summon the courage and energy required to make drastic changes.

For anger to be useful, people must do more than merely experience the feeling. Those whom anger motivates productively undergo a four-step process. First, they feel the anger. Second, they recognize the situation that provoked it. Then they identify a healthy, productive goal that would alleviate the situation. And finally, they maintain the anger until they can take the first steps toward the goal.

Psychological Protection

Mrs. Jones grew up in a family with seven brothers and sisters. Her father left the family when she was eight. Her mother did odd jobs, which were sometimes demeaning, in order to provide the basic necessities for her family without help from the Welfare Department. Mrs. Jones strongly holds to the belief that welfare is for those who need it.

Mrs. Jones and her husband, both aged fifty-eight, have been together now for thirty-eight years. They have worked hard, providing for two children and gathering some amenities of the middle-class life. Although her husband was unfortunately unable to work during the winter owing to ill health, Mrs. Jones continued with her job. But clerical work didn't pay enough to cover all their bills. They applied for and received fuel assistance from the New England city where they lived.

One morning, Mrs. Jones read in the local paper that the mayor, in an attempt to reduce the budget by lowering the fuel-assistance allotment, had said, "Only those who are too lazy to work ask for fuel assistance." Mrs. Jones was irate. The mayor's comment hit at the core of her values. She had always taken pride in being a hard worker. It was a piece of her self-image that she was willing to defend, and defend it she did. She wrote a pointed letter to the mayor, who invited her for a meeting. Once in his office, she refused to move until he retracted his statement publicly. The next morning the paper ran the mayor's apology.

Mrs. Jones's response demonstrates what is perhaps anger's most important function for modern people: the protection of personal dignity, identity, and self-esteem. When a person thinks she is being put down, ignored, ridiculed, or victimized, anger is likely to occur. This feeling encourages the individual to stand up for self and defend against being cheated, belittled, or emotionally attacked. It is the piece of self that says, "You don't have the right to treat me that way."

Not only is anger not dangerous, it is useful. The human body needs this mechanism. A person needs the ability to protect herself from physical and verbal attacks. When her solitary power is inadequate for this protection, she needs to bond with others to gain the necessary additional strength. No emotion or human characteristic other than anger performs these functions. This fact being true, how has anger earned a reputation as the trigger for harm and destruction? Like an ax, anger is not inherently destructive. It has many possible functions. But if a person doesn't learn the many aspects of proper use, the results can be disastrous. To avoid the possible harmful effects, anger must be understood. What are the triggers for healthy anger? What does productive anger look like? How can it be used constructively?

CHAPTER THREE

Acknowledging the Complexities of Anger

Human beings are the only creatures on earth that can think about, process, and understand their feelings. Only they contemplate and judge their emotions and resultant behaviors. Cats can't; horses can't; chimps can't. Even my dog, the companion I think is so intelligent, can't. She doesn't think about why her hair stands on end when she barks viciously at the little schnauzer next door. And she certainly doesn't return home, sit in her favorite chair, and think, "Jeez, I'm a real bully, picking on a dog half my size." She feels and acts solely out of instinct. She can't abstract or think about her feelings. But human beings can and do.

As a person goes through each day, his mind is constantly working: gathering new information, adding it to the old, rearranging this data, and drawing conclusions. The results can be acted upon immediately or set aside and possibly used at a future time. Ironically, this process that sets people apart and above other animals also impedes the productive use of emotions, especially anger. If the human brain were as simple as an animal's, emotions would be clear and action automatic. Because of its complexity, many pieces must all operate properly together for anger to work constructively.

An Emotion Is Only One Element of a Process

Some noted researchers argue that anger and aggressive behaviors are instinctive and biologically based. Other observers, just as noteworthy, adamantly contend that aggression is not instinctive, but a problem-solving technique learned from imitation of role-models.[1] Both groups back up their views with valid studies. How can both findings be true when there is such an apparent conflict?

What reconciles the disparity is the fact that people today are a product of evolution; the instinctive component of aggression, studied by some researchers, lies in the primitive area of the brain. That component comes into play when a person's physical well-being or that of another is at stake. The response from the "old brain" involves only a minor amount of mental activity except recognition of a present danger and automatic mobilization of the body's survival mechanism. The process is similar to my dog's experience in an emergency: recognition of danger, intense fear, the need to fight (anger), and the fight itself (aggression).

The other group of researchers studied the anger and aggression that originates in the "new brain" or neocortex functions. Since this part of the brain analyzes, learns, and abstracts, it operates on thought, not instinct. These researchers therefore concluded that anger and aggression are a cognitive, imitative process.

Instinct cannot and need not change. It is not people's instinctive aggression that causes problems. In today's society, a minority of individuals encounter situations in which their physical survival is at stake, when the primitive brain activates. Most confusion about anger and what people do with it concerns the anger generated by the neocortex, the topic of this book.

Any discussion of anger begins with an investigation of emotions in general and their resultant behaviors. Earlier, an emotion was defined as an internal reaction, which an individual learns to name, to an external event. This description states what a feeling is, not how it arose or how it is expressed. The feeling itself is neither the beginning event nor the end result. It is one element, the emotional piece, of a complex process, which also includes mental and behavioral components. Figure A depicts how the components work together in this process.

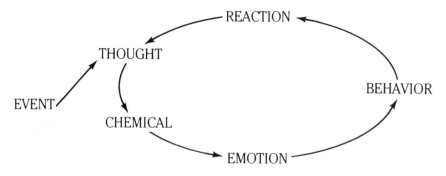

Figure A

This diagram suggests the circular character of an emotion's incitement, its presence as an experience, and its expression. What the drawing omits is the enormous input and learning from many sources which are necessary for the process.

Event

Something happens that signals the brain. This event may seem as insignificant as the smell of fresh coffee or a grumbled "Good morning" from a co-worker. Even a memory of a previous situation, something that happened earlier in the day, or yesterday, or years ago, may set off the process.

Thought

Once the event is sensed, the brain interprets the event. The person's current perception is influenced by past experiences, the lessons he learned from those situations, and his understanding of the present social setting. Often an individual must possess both an array of experiences and knowledge of social norms to interpret an event accurately.

    If the event is a memory, this assessment has already been made, but the mental revival of the situation may develop new insight and change the earlier interpretation. Whether the event originates internally or externally, from all of this mental activity, a predominant thought emerges.

Chemical

The brain responds to this thought by signaling the body to produce a chemical.

Emotion

The released chemical creates a physiological sensation, which the individual recognizes as a particular feeling.

Behavior

The person then chooses a behavior. This choice isn't simple. It coordinates all the information gathered during the interpretation process with the signal sent by the physiological sensation. The emotion is labeled. Then the brain quickly scans the array of behaviors available and the person acts.

    Many factors determine what behavioral choices a person has developed. No two people have the same range of options. Children learn behaviors by watching and imitating significant people. The acquisition of knowledge and experience modifies those behaviors, modifications which are especially important when one judges the socially acceptable response to a situation.

Reaction

The behavior a person chooses affects the other people who are present, who react in turn.

If no one is present when the behavior occurs, or if the event is internal, the reaction happens in the person's own mind. She judges and responds to her own behavior. I once received a phone call from a potential client whose opening line was, "I understand you know something about anger." As we talked and she explained her reasons for calling, I found out that she had just felt enraged over an incident with a friend. Being alone, she looked around for something to throw. When she couldn't find anything substantial, she slammed the door of the wood stove with such force that its glass window broke. I asked what she was telling herself about that behavior. In other words, what was her reaction to herself. She said, "I destroy everything. I hate it. I want to run away."

Event

The reaction constitutes another event, and the circle continues.

Although this process appears very complicated, it plays out in everyday situations so fluidly and instantaneously that we hardly notice: you step out onto your front porch on the first spring-like day of the year. A soft breeze brushes your face. You take a deep breath and smell the fresh odor of moist earth *(Event)*. Your mind responds, "Pretty day" *(Thought)*. A chemical is released that produces a nice sensation throughout your body. You feel glad *(Emotion)*. Going to your car, you smile and nod hello to the mail carrier *(Behavior)*. He smiles and nods back *(Reaction/Event)*. "He's a nice guy," you think *(Thought)*. This positive outlook and resultant feeling persists as you drive to work. Even the minor traffic jams don't bother you. You turn the car radio to your favorite music and reinforce the experience.

When you arrive at work, your spouse calls to tell you that your brother has been in a car accident *(Event)*.

Your mind springs to a picture of a badly wrecked automobile, and you think, "John's in that wreckage" *(Thought)*. Adrenaline begins to flow. Your body temperature starts to rise, and you feel shaky. Your hands are wet.

You're afraid *(Emotion)*. In a voice a little higher pitched than normal, you ask, "Is John all right?" *(Behavior)*.

Your spouse says, "Oh, yes. Somehow he ended up with only a few cuts and bruises" *(Reaction/Event)*.

You think, "He's okay" *(Thought)*. The chemicals change and you feel relief *(Emotion)*. Exhaling a deep sigh, you say, "Thank God!" *(Behavior)*.

This circular process continues for the rest of the day, every minute of the day, until you sleep.

How Anger Fits into the Process

Once the circular process of a feeling is understood, the next logical step is to place anger into the process and treat it like any other emotion. For years, that's what I did. In my training, I had learned that the behavior most constructive for mental and emotional health is the free expression of intense emotions. Such expression, I had learned, permits relief from hurtful emotions and enables the development of deeper, more meaningful interpersonal relationships. During my years as a counselor, I found that this assumption is true about the feelings of fear, loneliness, sadness, and guilt. But when anger is involved, I noticed the opposite result. People back away from the person who expresses anger. Relationships don't become deeper or closer. On the contrary, the involved people separate further.

Despite this realization, I had two reasons for continuing to encourage people to express anger freely. Anger is a feeling, and I believe that the sharing of feelings leads to more substantial relationships. I also had bought into the "reservoir theory": a person doesn't let anger out, but carries it around, adding new supplies each time anger occurs and remains unexpressed; eventually it overflows in the form of an aggressive, violent explosion. Ventilation lowers the level of the reservoir and averts violence.

In 1980, when I was asked to train professionals to help angry clients, I researched the subject. I wanted to back up my theories with other professionals' techniques and the results from studies.

As I read over a hundred articles, research studies, and books, I found that many counseling professionals held beliefs similar to my own and were acting accordingly. But the research didn't always support our practices. Below is a synopsis of information I gathered from studies. It helps explain the ingredients and process necessary for an individual to use anger as a positive, functional aspect of the personality.

• Ventilation correlates significantly with greater physical aggression.[2]

- Catharsis does not reduce the physiological arousal of anger.[3]

- The physiological arousal of anger is reduced by physical motor activity.[4]

- Verbally discharged anger is used to remove threats and obstructions.[5]

- Anger protects integrity and self-identity. Put-downs are the most frequent incitement of angry feelings.[6]

- Anger is always accompanied by anxiety. Anger acts as a defense against that anxiety.[7]

- High self-disclosure, followed by personal threat, is a powerful elicitor of anger.[8]

- Assertiveness training reduces aggression.[9]

- Fear and anger are mechanisms that protect, one by escape and the other with the desire to attack.[10]

- Anger is created by both environmental and imagined cues. The person evaluates these cues, forms a value judgment, and makes an accusation.[11]

This summary of information concerning the productive use of anger suggests the complexity of the emotion. In some ways, it performs differently from other emotions. Its constructive use requires more than the circular formula of *feeling it and letting it out, feeling it again and letting it out again*. A person would be trapped in this cycle forever; according to the studies on ventilation and catharsis, the anger and resultant behavior become more intense with each turn through the cycle. The reservoir of anger, if it exists, becomes larger, not smaller. Other people move further and further away.

Emotion

Figure B, a linear adaptation of the circle diagram, depicts the process of constructive anger. It occurs after the body experiences the adrenaline-produced sensation of fear, which could be recognized as nervousness, anxiety, or insecurity. When the individual can't avoid the fear-invoking situation, or if angry feelings would produce a gain for the individual, the emotion changes to anger. It functions to protect against whatever object, situation, or person is creating the fear. Anyone who has been cut off by a careless driver and has responded with anger knows how quickly this phenomenon can occur.

A dotted line crosses the feeling area of the diagram between anger and fear. Since anger is an emotion, it belongs in this area. But it is never a *primary* emotion. It is always secondary to fear or anxiety. This fact explains why anger differs from other feelings. Its main function is to protect and build walls. It masks another emotion, it defends, and therefore, its performance more closely matches that of a defense mechanism than that of a feeling. For this reason, shared anger doesn't bring antagonists closer together, catharsis doesn't reduce anger arousal, and ventilation doesn't diminish the intensity of angry feelings.

In fact, the opposite occurs. Any defense used, whether it be rationalization, projection, or outright denial, hides feelings and keeps other people at an emotional distance. If a person were to wallow around in that defense or have it validated through the ventilation process, it would become more prevalent in her character and more strongly entrenched. The results would be greater inability to experience the hidden feelings and increased emotional distance in relationships with others.

I have observed another characteristic of defenses which I have not seen investigated in the research. When a defense is used to its utmost effect, and then stretched further, if another defense doesn't take over immediately, the feelings underneath pour forth. A friend at her mother's funeral was laughing and joking to hide her sadness. After about half an hour, she suddenly stopped in the middle of a laugh and began sobbing. Her defense of laughter had been stretched beyond its limit.

All of the reactions described above apply as well to anger, including the last. Many times I have watched a person's anger heighten rapidly until it reached its limit, broke away, and left the person shaking and crying as the fear, which lay beneath, surfaced.

The fact that anger acts as a defense mechanism doesn't mean it is not an emotion. It involves a physiological response, which can be labeled, to an external event. It prepares the body to ward off an attack. That is the function of this emotion. To try to make anger fit the mold and react like other feelings denies its very character.

So far, anger of the neocortex seems similar to that of the old brain. Born of fear, it functions to protect and defend. It differs from the instinctive response in *what* it protects and *how* it defends.

Thought

The neocortex abstracts and produces symbols. That ability enables human beings to form a concept of self and to determine how that self fits into the immediate environment and, at times, the rest of the world. This idea of self, whether it be called self-concept, self-image, or self-identity, begins developing shortly after birth and is composed of positive and negative evaluations provided by a child's significant people. Very early in life, a child internalizes these judgments from others as if he had made them himself. After a harsh reprimand, a child thinks, "I'm bad," instead of the more realistic thought, "Mother said I'm bad." After praise, the child thinks, "I'm good," not the more accurate description, "The teacher likes the way I read." In this process, a conception of the self develops. This image remains into adulthood. Being the basis for personal evaluation, it colors interpretations of external events.

When a person has many more positive self-evaluations than negative ones, an affirming self-concept evolves. He sees self as a good person, on equal footing with other people, worthwhile as a human being, deserving of personal rights. The concept of self as a valued piece of humanity is affirmed. It is neither an inflated nor deflated evaluation of self. It isn't about being better or worse than others. It affirms the idea, "As a person, I am equal. I belong. I am not above others in a godlike posture, nor am I below others, filling a subhuman role."

An affirming self-concept furnishes a sense of adequacy, a general, overall feeling of being equipped to handle the events each day may bring. It provides self-esteem. It engenders the soft dignity that allows the person to make mistakes without the shame of self-deprecation.

Anger's role is to protect this sense of adequacy from situations and events that are perceived as threats to the affirming self-concept. And because an individual with this realistic perspective of self has a realistic view of the events in her life, these threats are accurately perceived and the resultant anger is appropriate to the situation.

CONSTRUCTIVE ANGER

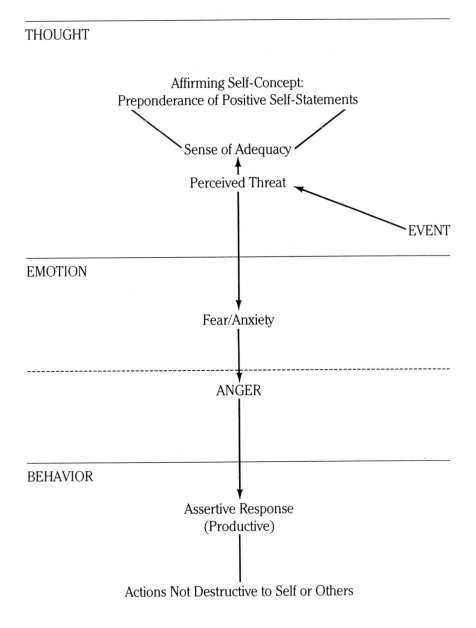

THOUGHT

Affirming Self-Concept:
Preponderance of Positive Self-Statements

Sense of Adequacy

Perceived Threat

EVENT

EMOTION

Fear/Anxiety

ANGER

BEHAVIOR

Assertive Response
(Productive)

Actions Not Destructive to Self or Others

Figure B

Behavior

The lower part of the model depicting behavior shows that, once anger is aroused, it defends most effectively when the individual employs an assertive response. This type of response neither attacks nor retreats, but holds firm. It states fact and feeling. It allows the anger to be heard in the person's tone of voice and seen in the person's facial expression. It describes the situation as perceived and indicates what the person needs for that situation to change. It then requires that the person follow through to obtain those needs. If those needs aren't met initially, the individual uses the anger to develop another plan to assert self. No matter how many attempts are required, the person with an affirming self-concept persists until she preserves her sense of human adequacy.

With constructive anger, people do not choose behaviors with the purpose of resolving the anger. Problems need resolution. Anger, functioning normally, is not a problem. It is a tool that protects a person's self-image. Once the affirming self-concept and the sense of adequacy are free from threat, the anger, no longer necessary, dissipates.

Taken as a whole, the linear model of healthy anger shows the many components of a complex process. A person with self-esteem, seeing that his sense of adequacy is threatened, initially feels fear and anxiety. Because there is no need or means to avoid the situation, or because standing firm in the situation is more advantageous, this feeling changes to anger. The individual then chooses and acts out a behavior that protects his self-concept but won't harm others or self.

I remember the day my friend Bob, an accountant, came to my house, shaking with anger. In fact, his fury was so intense that it took a while for him to get his story out. His superior earlier that afternoon had belittled him for an omission in one of his accounts. Bob had made the mistake because that same supervisor had failed to give him valuable information.

Bob went on to tell me that a similar situation had occurred ten days before. At that time, he had defended himself by expressing his displeasure about the criticism, especially for something not his fault. He had said that he didn't want such a thing to happen again, but now it had. Bob sputtered with anger, "It didn't work. What do I do now? I can't just leave. I have bills to pay."

Although my friend had some understanding of assertiveness, he had missed two important points. People don't change just because we ask; in fact, people don't change even when we demand. Moreover, an assertive response is often more than an event. Instead, it is a program of actions in which one behavior lays the foundation for the next, and that one for the next, and so on. The person becomes assertive by taking that first step and remains so throughout the process.

By the end of the evening, Bob and I had rewritten his resume. The next day he mailed out copies to twenty firms in the area. Within six weeks, he had a new job and a new supervisor who didn't unfairly criticize him.

These results confirmed his self-concept, his knowledge that he is a person deserving respect.

An individual who is having problems with anger can change her process and learn to use anger constructively. Before she can achieve this goal, however, she needs to know the cause of the problems. Is it the building of a reservoir that eventually and continually overflows? I wish it were that simple. It would make the remedy easy: reduce the amount by letting the anger out. But anger by definition is the physiological sensation created by the production of adrenaline in the body. To state that an individual has a large supply of anger (a reservoir) is the same as saying she carries around an extra supply of adrenaline twenty-four hours a day. That is impossible.

Another invalidation of the reservoir idea is the fact that angry feelings can easily be reduced by physical activity, which reduces the adrenaline. Nevertheless, because the emotion is only one piece of the process, the anger will certainly return.

If the reservoir theory isn't the answer, what is? What blocks a person from gaining access to and using the anger experience in a way that not only doesn't harm self or others, but affirms self and respects others?

CHAPTER FOUR

Understanding How Anger Goes Awry

Jack seems to walk around with a chip on his shoulder, at the ready to con-
tradict and argue. Darlene is always smiling, even on days following her husband's drunken episodes, when he has repeatedly degraded her. Carla is shy
and retiring, spending most of her time doing for others, and then complain-
ing constantly to her sister about how people use her. Jason loses his temper
at the drop of a hat. These people are unable to use angry feelings to enrich
their lives. Instead, the anger has turned against them and become a vehicle
of pain. To discover how this distortion of nature happens, one must understand the many ways people can lose their ability to use any emotion for its
intended function. Then, by combining this information with research findings and applying the results to anger specifically, it is possible to see how the
anger process goes awry.

How Emotions Become Distorted

Understanding the circular process of emotions and describing it on paper
may make it seem easy. Obviously it isn't. Many people have difficulty experiencing and expressing their emotions. The fact is that problems may impair
any element of the process and, because it is circular, disrupt it throughout.

Thought

My description of the emotional process crucially assumes that the interpretation of the event coincides with reality—not the subjective reality of the in-

dividual, but objective reality. When perceptions are skewed, when a person's defense mechanisms distort and limit his ability to interpret life events accurately, the range of emotional experiences diminishes, behavioral options are fewer, and reactions from others have a greater tendency to be negative. The person applies another distorted interpretation to these reactions, and the process continues, becoming progressively deformed.

Because the interpretation of an event develops from personal experience, misinterpretations are common. I once asked a worker whom I supervised to come into my office. She looked panic-stricken. I asked what was going on, and she replied, "I didn't do anything wrong." I told her that, on the contrary, I wanted to offer her a promotion. She appeared shocked. As we talked, she explained that, in the past, being called into the supervisor's office meant a reprimand.

Chemical

Anything that disrupts the body's chemical balance directly affects a person's emotional state because it determines physiological sensation. In fact, serious chemical disruptions create major illnesses such as depression and schizophrenia. The reverse is also true: PMS and such diseases as diabetes cause major chemical imbalances. These illnesses produce extreme emotions and require medical treatment.

Some of the other influences on a person's chemical make-up include diet, stress, resting habits, and exercise. An individual who begins to experience intense feelings that seem unrelated to real situations or events may find the cause in such factors.

Prescription and nonprescription drugs also interrupt the natural production and release of body chemicals. When my friend Richard began taking prescribed steroids for a medical condition, he experienced mood swings that ranged from deep sadness to overwhelming anger. He cried uncontrollably one minute and broke things the next. He thought he was going crazy. His doctor sent him to a psychiatrist, who explained that steroids cause emotional instability in some people.

Because of the nature and seriousness of Richard's illness, the steroids unfortunately could not be stopped or exchanged for another medication. But much of his anxiety was reduced when he understood what was happening. Anyone taking prescription drugs who finds that mood swings are suddenly a problem should contact the prescribing physician. Another drug may be available that doesn't have this side effect; or the dosage of the medication may need to be modified.

Over-the-counter medications may also affect mood. Any substance that contains caffeine or causes drowsiness as a side effect is especially likely to produce emotional changes.

Alcohol and illegal drugs interfere with the chemical balance of the body. Indeed, the sole purpose of using them is to change moods. Regular use of these substances may result in episodes of depression, hostility, or anxiety. Excessive use produces these same emotional states with greater frequency and more intensity. Such a case necessitates an evaluation and counsel by a professional who specializes in substance abuse.

Emotion

In most cultures, taboos forbid certain feelings and their expression. The culture determines which emotions are acceptable. For instance, some boys are taught that men aren't supposed to cry. Many times I've heard a parent say to a son, "Now be a man, don't cry." To suppress an emotion, especially if he feels it intensely, requires the child to hide it from himself. The child develops a mental defense system that tells him he doesn't feel sad. The strength of this system determines how much sadness he can feel. The sadness is there, but his thinking won't *allow* him to experience the physiological sensation.

Other taboos restrict the social acceptability of openly experiencing an emotion. A feeling may be all right to have at a party, but not at work. If it occurs at work, it must be concealed. Masked too often, the feeling becomes hidden, even from the person carrying it.

Some adults who grew up in a family that prohibited most emotions and their expression are unable to label feelings. In childhood, such a person rarely saw significant adults express certain feelings. When forbidden feelings did arise, they were assigned the name of a more "acceptable" feeling. As an adult, this individual continues to attach incorrect labels to these feelings, a habit that results in isolation and obstruction of intimacy. Other people, viewing the mislabeled feelings as inappropriate to the situation, back away, not only emotionally, but physically as well.

Behavior

Most behavioral patterns develop during childhood and then are modified by experiences throughout adolescence and adulthood. A child observes significant adults. She imitates their interactions and incorporates into her own range of possible behaviors the adults' ways of resolving conflicts and problems. If these behaviors are ineffective, then the child responds ineffectively throughout her life, unless she somehow expands her repertoire. She may wonder why things don't work out, or why other people get all the breaks.

The number of behaviors, effective or ineffective, accessible to an individual are very limited if significant adults have displayed only a few options. As the child grows older and begins interacting with others outside the family setting, she lacks the behaviors necessary to cope with a multitude of varying situations.

This same problem of limited behavioral choices also occurs when adults, out of love and the need to protect, try to insulate children from painful but normal life events. A child who isn't allowed to attend funerals, for instance, will not know how to act at a funeral when he grows up.

Another limiting behavioral condition exists when a person was raised in a family that provided an array of behavioral choices, but he has lacked the opportunities to expand and modify these choices through life experiences. This modification process involves skills developed by practice. It involves recognizing nuances in a present situation, and rearranging an old behavior to fit the new necessity. If a person lacks diversity in life experience, he may not even be aware that circumstances require new or modified behaviors. This obliviousness often happens when a person steps from one culture to another, or from one social class to another. At a social gathering, he employs familiar behaviors that were acceptable in past circumstances but now violate the new group's norms. At a formal dinner for contributors to our scholarship fund, I saw a guest cringe as he watched my coworker use bread to sop up the gravy on his plate, a behavior acceptable in another setting.

Reaction

The reaction behavior of others from the external environment affects one's internal emotional circle. When a person spends most of her time with others who are kind, honest, and positive, the feedback is of this nature, and her internal response follows suit. The child who is told repeatedly that she is pretty begins to believe it. The worker who is acknowledged for merit, sees self as worthy.

On the other hand, if the people surrounding her are sarcastic, manipulative, and judgmental, the events in the environment become a negative barrage, producing an abundance of hurtful feelings. To survive emotionally, the individual must use defenses often. The more often defenses are used, the harder they are to turn off. They carry over into other situations where they are not needed, distorting the interpretation of events. A person who spends a great deal of time with a sarcastic group of people expects to hear sarcasm, not only from them, but also from others. Because of her expectation, she hears sarcasm when people don't intend it. She even hears silent sarcasm from herself. This misunderstanding results in distortions in thought.

Research about Destructive Anger

Nancy, a counselor at a treatment center, attended a Weekend Anger Clinic that I facilitated. When asked what prompted her to show up at a twenty-hour group about anger, she explained that her friends continually told her that she looked angry and defensive.

She went on to say, "Even when I'm working with clients and I think I'm showing them that I care, they say I'm loud and harsh. I don't feel angry then. When I am angry, I pout."

Nancy's anger was destructive. It was hurting those she tried to help, affecting her competency as a counselor, and damaging her social relationships. How had the variables that distort emotions affected the anger process in such a way that her anger had become so hurtful?

To answer this question, we need to go to the research findings, which provide some clues on the development of anger, not as a tool for protection but as a pain-producing weapon. Below is a synopsis of these findings:

• Aggression is a response to frustration.[1]

• Aggression is a learned problem-solving technique.[2]

• There is a strong cultural factor in aggression.[3]

• Aggression is most likely to occur when the chance of painful consequences is low.[4]

• Violence is a way of overcoming a strong sense of worthlessness and helplessness.[5]

• Anger is tied to self-identity.[6]

• People remember experiences of threat, anxiety, and anger.[7]

• Both depression and anger are strongly influenced by the irrational belief that external events create happiness and problems.[8]

• Both angry and depressed people blame their situation and feelings on others.[9]

• People with a diagnosis of depression have explosive episodes of aggression.[10]

• Fear, anger, and depression are somehow linked.[11]

• There is a difference between anger and hostility, and between anger and violence. Anger is equated with these other manifestations because they often occur together.[12]

One finding deserves special attention and discussion. A 1986 self-reporting survey of prisoners convicted of violent crimes shows that 53.5 percent admitted to being under the influence of alcohol, drugs, or a combination when they committed the acts for which they were imprisoned.[13] This statistic is probably low. Since it is a self-reporting survey, it requires that the respondents answer honestly, and some may be unwilling to admit to alcohol and drug use.

Even if this statistic is accurate, 53.5 percent is a strong indication that alcohol and other drugs are variables in violent behavior. At the very least, they are potentiating ingredients of extreme aggression that cannot be ignored. Nothing can change a person's anger patterns when alcohol or other drugs are involved until the chemical use stops. These chemicals cloud the thought process. They distort reality and impair judgment. They radically interfere with the body's chemical make-up.

If you are reading this because you or someone you care about is having difficulty with anger, consider whether alcohol or other drugs are involved. If the answer is yes, please put this manual aside and go to a substance-abuse professional. Further reading can bring about no benefit until the chemical use stops.

How Anger Becomes Destructive

The research findings and the variety of ways feelings can be affected suggest that the distortion of healthy anger is a complex and gradual process. (Figure C demonstrates this fact.)

People don't live in isolation. The importance and magnitude of culture and its effects upon an individual's inner life cannot be overestimated. People learn and transmit cultural norms through small social groups (family, church, school, peers, and others) that adapt the larger society's patterns, customs, and beliefs to their specific needs. This cultural training begins before a child can speak and is so pervasive that people pay as little attention to it as they do to the air they breathe. Yet nothing has a greater impact on the individual's experience and use of anger than this one variable; from these miniature societies, an individual learns about emotions, self, and acceptable behaviors.

When I talked with Nancy, the counselor who was not aware of her own anger, I asked what her parents had done when they became angry at her for doing something wrong. This information suggested the attitudes she had learned about anger. She talked mostly about her mother, who would ignore her, sometimes for as long as a week. How this one behavior affected Nancy's ability to feel and express angry feelings will be pointed out as I discuss how the components of anger go awry.

Emotion

Our culture promulgates many false tenets about fear and anger. When integrated into a person's response pattern, these beliefs create problems. Probably as many misconceptions about fear and anger exist as there are human beings. One of the most common is the idea that *anger is an accusation* and is equivalent to disapproval of the human person. Someone with this perspective has to see self as right, and the target of the anger arousal as wrong, for this emotion to be acceptable. At an extreme, he must set about methodically proving the other's wrongness. His anger is therefore very judgmental, leaving little room for mistakes from self or others. The flip side is also true: he interprets other people's anger as finger-pointing and accusatory, an evaluation of his personal worth.

To a greater or lesser degree, most parents teach this misconception about anger without realizing the lesson they are instilling. When do parents express anger toward a child? The answer is obvious: when the child has made a mistake, done wrong, or failed to follow directions. There is nothing inappropriate about a parent's expressing anger as long as the child is not accused of having caused the emotion and as long as the message is clear that the *behavior* is wrong, not the child.

When her mother was angry, Nancy was treated as a nonperson. She learned that she had caused her mother's anger and that anger is hurtful.

Another false view society teaches is the idea that *anger is bad* and the person who feels it is a bad person. Adults teach this lesson very easily with phrases like "Don't be angry," or with words spoken in a derogatory tone of voice: "Oh, him. He's an angry person." The message is clear: something is wrong with this emotion and with the person who has it.

Since moving from New England to the South eighteen years ago, I have encountered the mistaken belief, taught by some churches' doctrine, that *anger is a sin.* When I inquired about the theory behind this belief, people explained that anger is the opposite of love and that it interferes with a person's ability to love. Therefore, anger is a sin because it blocks the love that God wants us to feel.

I do not have the expertise to argue about what God wants. I *can* argue that anger and love are not opposites and that anger does not interfere with love. Indeed, anger is an integral part of love. There is no need to look far to understand what I mean. The relationship between a mother and her child illustrates the point. Think of how strong and unconditional that love is, and yet, each mother I have talked to agrees that her angriest moments involve her children.

Many people have learned that *anger is dangerous.* A child who has watched an angry father batter his mother, who has received physical pun-

THOUGHT

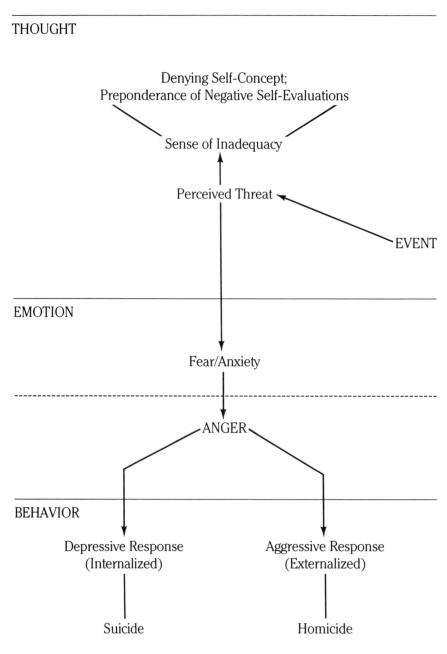

Denying Self-Concept;
Preponderance of Negative Self-Evaluations

Sense of Inadequacy

Perceived Threat

EVENT

EMOTION

Fear/Anxiety

ANGER

BEHAVIOR

Depressive Response
(Internalized)

Aggressive Response
(Externalized)

Suicide

Homicide

Figure C

ishment as discipline, or who has incurred harsh emotional abuse from angry parents, has learned that, when someone is angry, someone else gets hurt. Anger is then seen as a weapon of revenge, pain, and punishment. It is harmful. It is a danger to be avoided. It is violent.

Nancy's mother taught her this lesson. Ignoring a child, for a short time, let alone a long time, is emotional abuse. Nurturance is as vital to a child's emotional well-being as food is to her physical health.

Our culture inculcates other erroneous views about emotions that affect the anger process, such as *fear is wrong*. This piece of misinformation is usually held by a person who believes that feelings are divided into two categories: good and bad. Good feelings are those deemed pleasant. Bad feelings are all the rest. These groups are mutually exclusive, and only feelings from the pleasant category are acceptable. The others aren't allowed. Fear is almost always placed in the "bad" category.

Parents, teachers, and friends imply this falsehood every time they try to remove fear from someone by saying, "There's nothing to be afraid of—it won't hurt," or, "Don't be nervous; it'll be okay." The idea comes across that to be nervous or scared is not okay.

The idea that *men don't feel afraid* distorts countless personalities in our culture. Feshback's study not only showed that children learn to label feelings by the age of six, but that a significant number of boys could not label fear.[14] I am convinced that, at an early age, boys learn that fear is not a manly emotion. Cowards and sissies are afraid; men are not. This attitude used to be called the "John Wayne Syndrome," a term that can now be updated to the "Rambo Syndrome."

"Be a big boy; face it like a man," are the words spoken to many a small child. They mean, "hide your fear; don't feel it." Probably the fathers of such children rarely, if ever, demonstrate their fear, a flatness which reinforces the lesson.

A concomitant of the damaging emotional rule about men and fear is the prohibition that *ladies don't get angry*. There is something socially unacceptable about a woman who openly expresses anger.[15] Even if she expresses her angry feelings appropriately, she is often labeled as aggressive, unfeminine, or tyrannical.

This particualar lesson is dear to me, since my mother verbalized it and demonstrated it. Despite what I know about anger, it is a hard lesson to overcome. Every time I feel angry, a twinge of inadequacy shoots through me. I am sure that, at that moment, I just flunked "ladyhood."

Many people recognize their angry feelings but then attempt to distance themselves from those feelings by means of the misconception that *another person is responsible*. Something or someone else has caused the anger sensation. This untruth is so strong that it becomes a two-way channel: you're responsible for my angry feelings, and I'm responsible for yours. My anger is your fault and your anger is my fault. For my physiological sensation of adrenaline to be reduced, you must change. And for yours to diminish I must change.

Blaming anger on another person is so common that it has become incorporated into our language: "You make me angry." Even professionals who teach communication skills help to keep this misinformation going as they train their students to say, "I feel angry because/when you do that." The word "because" places direct blame for the anger on the other person. The word "when" implies another clear message: "When you stop, my anger will go away. The responsibility for its starting and stopping is yours." Though Nancy's mother never said a word about her angry feelings, the message was clear. Nancy was to blame.

The assimilation of such misinformation as these cultural tenets into a person's feeling life results in distortions, a limited range of emotions, or a lack of feeling. Belief in these ideas requires the individual to deny and avoid the feelings. The consequence is an inability to feel, reverse labeling and unclear labeling, and adoption of the victim posture.

The *inability to feel* develops when a person believes that angry feelings are so bad that they must be avoided at any cost. To some extent Nancy experienced this problem. Her friends could see her anger, even when she didn't know she was feeling it.

Since anger is an intense physiological sensation, a strong defense system of denial must be developed to keep it hidden. This system is so firmly entrenched and deeply rooted that feelings less intense than anger are also masked, not only from others but also from self. The person who cannot feel angry also loses the ability to experience the physiological sensations responsible for fear, guilt, and joy. Nancy couldn't show feelings of care to her clients.

In this state, the emotional tools needed for effective living—feelings—are inaccessible. The fear that signals potentially dangerous situations becomes "invisible." The anger required to stand firm is absent.

Reverse labeling occurs when someone believes that anger is okay, but fear is bad. Both feelings spring from the same physiological sensation. Eventually, therefore, whenever the sensation occurs, he labels it anger.[16] Fear or anxiety might be the more appropriate label for the situation, but anger is more acceptable. He vehemently denies being afraid of anything. The denial is honest. He doesn't know his initial adrenaline sensation originates in fear. He seems intensely angry because he is using the "anger" label to denote two emotions instead of one, and he acts accordingly.

The opposite phenomenon also happens. Someone who finds fear more acceptable tends to stay with that label when the adrenaline of anger is released. She escapes and avoids when she might more advantageously stand firm. She feels a level of fear that seems excessive for the occasion.

Unclear labeling occurs when someone can feel the sensation but has been taught that more acceptable labels than "anger" or "fear" attach to it. These labels include, but are not limited to, "upset," "bored," "tired of," "hurt," and "disappointed." There is nothing inherently incorrect about these words. Unfortunately, they aren't specific enough to clarify which sensation is being felt. To me, "upset" means terribly sad; to someone else, it means "angry"; to another, "afraid." These labels lead to emotional confusion in the person who uses them and misunderstanding in those who hear them.

One of my experiences shows how people can fail to communicate. Somehow I have learned that "excited" means sexually aroused. I was working in an outpatient clinic on an especially hard day when my last client arrived. He was a sixty-seven-year-old man, balding and toothless. He wore a dirty coat and appeared not to have had a bath in quite a while. As I was confronting him about some of his inappropriate behaviors, he turned to me and said, "Lorrainne, you're getting me excited." My immediate thought was, "It's too late in the day to deal with this kind of thing." I still thank God that I asked my client for clarification and didn't respond according to my assumption about the meaning of "excited." What he was trying to tell me was that he felt angry.

The *victim posture*, the role taken by someone who sees self as emotional prey for others, is a direct result of misplacing responsibility for angry feelings. This individual focuses more on blaming others to channel the anger, or on changing others to reduce the anger, than on using the anger for protection and assertion of self.

Accepting responsibility for another's anger is also victimizing. Someone whose attention and effort are focused on others' feelings hasn't the energy to spend on personal wants and needs.

As Figure C illustrates, a person who experiences these problems is emotionally isolated from self and others. Deprived of the feelings information valuable to effective daily functioning, he cannot know how to express or respond to the masked emotions when they do surface.

Thought

When a person makes more negative than positive judgments of his character and personality, his self-concept revolves around denying the worthiness of self. Negative self-evaluations consist of short, judgmental statements such as, "I'm not important," "I'm not good enough," "I don't exist," "I'm wrong," and "I'm worthless." I have also heard (although not as often) "I'm a freak," "I'm a monster," "I'm awful."

Negative self-evaluations are instilled in children, whose minds are extremely impressionable. The judgments internalized during emotional trauma are the strongest and most dominant. A youngster who grows up with punishment and abuse experiences emotional trauma. At the same time she integrates the hurtful behaviors and statements she hears, accepting them as direct reflections of her worth. The result is a denying self-concept that will continue through adulthood. Thus a sensitive, talented artist hides his deepest secret, that he's a monster. A beautiful model thinks she is ugly.

What negative self-judgments had Nancy developed from her situation? She told me that when she was ignored, treated as a nonperson, she came to think, "I'm not here. I don't exist."

The person with a denying self-concept has a deep sense that he is defective. He holds a low estimate of his value as a human being, and responds to life in either a subhuman role or a godlike posture. In the first role, he lives on the outskirts of life, never expecting to be seen or recognized. In the second, he sees self as the center of the universe, absolutely convinced that everything that happens concerns him.

A denying self-concept creates a sense of inadequacy. A person who views reality through such a distorted glass finds a world filled with events that seem impossible to face. He experiences mistakes as deep wrongs that prove the accuracy of his hurtful self-image. Nothing the individual accomplishes is good enough, important enough, or worthy enough to relieve this felt inadequacy.

Since people hear, see, and communicate through the sieve of self-evaluations, someone who judges self inadequate expects and hears the same judgment from others. Each day, therefore, events pile up which he misinterprets as threatening.

A simple statement from his supervisor, "The data is missing," he translates as "You're incompetent" *(Negative self-evaluation)*. The adrenaline flows *(Chemical)* and anxiety begins *(Emotions)*. He avoids this vulnerable sensation by preparing to defend self. The anxiety changes to anger (a powerful sensation) as the thought, "Who does he think he is, talking to me that way!" resounds over and over again in his mind.

A "reservoir" that creates and feeds ineffective anger does indeed fill, but its contents are not anger. It is filled with skewed thinking. The reservoir contains a mounting supply of negative self-evaluations that feed the denying self-concept. The person with low self-esteem seems filled with anger because he interprets and responds in a defensive, angry way to events that objectively are nonthreatening. This behavior was habitual for Nancy. Since she was always ready to protect herself, her anger was always present, even when she wasn't aware of it.

Behavior

A person who feels a deep sense of inadequacy responds either aggressively or depressively, directing destructive anger outward or inward. Aggression is the response of an individual who externalizes anger. She knows she is angry and openly attacks others. The origin of this response, anger, is easy to recognize. The anger is visibly acted out. In fact, someone with this style incurs labels such as "hostile," "arrogant," and "defiant." Mild put-downs, biting sarcasm, verbal abuse, assault, and homicide are all aggressive behaviors. Each has its own degree of destructive potential. Each is a violent attack on the emotional or physical well-being of another person.

On the other side, depressive behaviors occur when a person is unaware of his angry thoughts and feelings and directs them inward toward self. This type of response is confusing because the behaviors mimic the symptoms of a chemical or biological depression. Even professional counselors have difficulty telling the difference. When depressive behaviors are severe, there is the chance that the individual is suffering from biological depression. Since this condition is an illness, it needs to be diagnosed and treated by the appropriate medical professionals. Often medications or other therapies can alleviate the symptoms rapidly.

Another confusing aspect of depressive responses is the difficulty in identifying anger as the source. Hidden even from self, it is often masked with "pleasant," socially acceptable defenses. The person may smile and laugh as though he were having a good time, while the physiological sensation of fear and anger rises.

Some less attractive defenses, such as self-pity, also hide underlying anger: "Poor me. I'm the one who always has to do the dishes when company comes" is a victim statement. A more accurate expression of feeling is, "I feel angry when I have to do dishes after company." Whining, a self-pitying activity, and gossip and backstabbing are behaviors that indicate anger. Pouting, Nancy's form of expression, is another unattractive defense that masks anger.

"Why" questions which clearly do not seek information are statements of anger turned around. For example, I was sitting in a friend's kitchen with her four-year-old daughter. The child spilled her milk. My friend walked in, stopped at the doorway, and asked the most ridiculous question I've ever heard: "Why'd you spill your milk?" Did she expect the youngster to respond,

"Well, Mom, I decided to knock my elbow against the glass so I could investigate the effects of gravity on solids and liquids"? This answer may seem ridiculous, but there is no sensible answer to the question because it is not meant to elicit a reply. My friend, in fact, turned around a different message: "I feel angry that I have to mop the floor."

Many parents use this form of noncommunication: "Why isn't your room clean?" "Why did you get an F on your report card?" or (my personal favorite) "Why did you hit your sister?" Think of the answers to those questions: "I didn't clean it," "I'm stupid," and "She's a jerk." A more accurate translation of each question is, "I'm angry about the fact that your room isn't clean," "I'm angry that you got an F," and "I'm angry about your hitting your sister."

Depressive behaviors occur in degrees of personal harm, such as mild put-downs to self, apathy, self-mutilation, inability to maintain life functions such as eating and hygiene, and suicide. Each of these behaviors is violent, attacking the emotional or physical well-being of self.

The aggressive and the depressive response styles are both destructive. The difference is the direction toward which the destruction is aimed. Usually nonassertive people use both styles to express anger, although one dominates more than the other. In situations when aggression has costly consequences, such as an argument at the office, a person is likely to internalize the anger. An hour later, when she feels angry at the children, consequences are low, and an aggressive response is more probable.

A small minority of people use one style or the other exclusively. These people eventually use the highest degree of destructiveness in the style. The reason for the increasing intensity is not that the anger arousal becomes so great that it overflows into an explosion or implosion. The intensity results from the ineffectiveness of behaviors that don't bring about desired results. When one ploy doesn't work, these people try another of the same style, but with greater intensity. The process continues until the final, destructive act.

Another group of people who act in extreme ways are those who have used one style exclusively for a long time. When that style continues to fail, and they are desperate for results, they switch to the other style. Being in unfamiliar territory, desperate, and not knowing how to use new behaviors, they act in extreme and often bizarre ways. I remember an instance of this behavior that occurred many years ago in Pennsylvania. A teenager came home from school and chopped up his mother and his sister with an axe. He then went to the park. The media interviewed the neighbors, asking, "What kind of boy was Johnny?" The answers: "He was the nicest kid, a Boy Scout. He never talked back. He was always willing to help. You'd never expect this from him." I would. It isn't normal for a teenager never to talk back, to be so nice and always helpful. Johnny never learned to assert self. When he finally tried, the result was extreme.

Every child learns behavioral response styles in her early home environment and modifies them as she grows older. A youngster learns to be aggressive when parents demonstrate that behavior as a means to get what they want. If it is the only response style used in front of the child, then it is the only response style learned. If a child hears sarcasm, then she learns sarcasm. When she witnesses violent behavior at home, she learns to be violent. A young person communicates with put-downs if the parents interact with put-downs.

If expressions of anger are taboo at home, then self-pity, whining, and gossip are the lessons learned. People-pleasing, which excludes the interest of the self, is taught. A child learns depressive responses by example and survival. She may learn the depressive response style through trial and error, as a survival necessity. In a violent home, the child learns that to express anger openly results in painful repercussions from the violent parent. Internalizing anger seems safer. The child practices this style, integrates it into her personality, and carries it on into adulthood.

The styles of both aggressive and depressive responses may be modified as life experience and knowledge increase. The more intense the original learning experience, the less likely are modifications. Unfortunately, the more intense learning experiences are those that involve the most violence.

Nancy's experience shows how distorted anger can result in depressive behaviors. Distorted anger, demonstrated aggressively, follows the same process. About four years ago, I worked as a consultant for a large city. As I walked through the city hall, I heard a loud voice and harsh words coming from an office (Aggressive Response). Being interested in this sort of thing, I decided to stop by. As I entered, the man in the office hung up the phone—in fact, he slammed it down.

I introduced myself and said, "Sounds bad, whatever it is." He launched into a tirade. "Don't they know I'm somebody!" (I'd wager a week's pay that he has a negative self-evaluation that is close to, if not precisely, "I'm nobody" or "I'm not important.") "They've reassigned the parking spaces and put me at the other end of the lot. *(Event)* I'm the Assistant Director. My space is near the door. That son of a bitch; I'll make his life miserable!" *(Thought)*

To find out whether someone wanted to undercut the Assistant Director's importance, I visited with the Department Director in charge of planning the parking lot. He told me that parking spaces had been reassigned to accommodate the field workers. Those who came and went frequently from the building were given the parking spaces closest to the doors.

The placement of a person's parking space is not a realistic threat to his adequacy as a human being. Someone with an affirming self-concept assumes that he is somebody and doesn't need a parking space to prove it.

When a person expresses anger destructively, whether with depressive behaviors or aggressive ones, people react negatively. Someone who is internalizing anger finds that others tend to avoid him. The same is true of a person who is aggressive. Most people avoid him, and some attack back. Whether people avoid or attack, the results are the same; the person's hurtful self-evaluations are validated and become stronger. His sense of inadequacy grows. The trap of destructive anger tightens.

The trap can be unlocked. Nancy did it. I was invited by her aftercare group to facilitate a discussion. At one point, I asked them how they would describe their counselor. There was a common theme; firm but fair, caring. Nancy grinned. I cried—as I always do when a person struggles and wins. I know the hard work she had done to earn that description. The Anger Clinic was only the beginning. She worked on exercises and continually practiced. Only with determination was she able to release herself from the grip of distorted anger.

CHAPTER FIVE

Changing Your Experience of Anger

Both my brother and I are natural swimmers. Growing up on the shore, we spent most of every summer's day in the water. We learned to swim without official training or much conscious effort. Our father, on the other hand, never had the opportunity to learn to swim when he was a child. We tried to teach him. We told him the principles and showed him the movements. Time and again, he tried and gave up. He may not have been a natural swimmer, but I'm convinced that if he had continued to try, he would have succeeded. Had he practiced his success, he could have become a good swimmer.

The same principle applies to anger. Some people are fortunate enough to have learned healthy anger skills during their childhood. As adults, they have access to these skills, which come naturally. Others, who didn't learn to develop methods to use angry feelings effectively, have to devise new behaviors, repeatedly try them, and as the successes occur, practice them.

This chapter presents exercises to help you use your anger productively.[1] Because the process of an emotion is circular, changes in any area of the anger process, whether it be in thoughts, emotions, or behaviors, produce changes in all areas. This fact allows you to choose where you want to begin.

I think the best results occur when a person becomes comfortable with his emotions, and so I recommend that you do the relaxation exercise and then begin with the exercises on emotions. Learn an exercise, try it out, and then practice it daily. In time, the skills engaged in constructive anger will become second nature.

Relaxation

Many of the exercises in this section require relaxation. You will therefore benefit (though it is not essential) from use of a tape recorder and a relaxation tape. When the exercise necessitates relaxation, go to a quiet place. Play the tape until you are relaxed and your mind is clear. Then proceed with the exercise.

If you don't have a relaxation tape, these steps are one way to relax:

1. Take a deep breath; hold it to the count of three.

2. Slowly let it out while mentally thinking the word "relax."

3. Take another deep breath; hold it to the count of three.

4. Slowly let it out while mentally thinking the word "relax."

5. Tighten both fists; count to three.

6. Open your fists and relax.

7. Take another deep breath; hold it to the count of three.

8. Slowly let it out while mentally thinking the word "relax."

Then proceed with the exercise.

Because anger is a product of anxiety, it can be helpful to reduce adrenaline during any stressful situation. This goal is easily accomplished by surreptitiously doing steps 1–4.

Emotions

Because anger is an emotion, it is important to become comfortable with feelings in general and then with anger specifically. Therefore, the first four exercises deal with feelings other than anger. I recommend that you work through this material before moving on.

Besides anger, humans experience only six basic emotions. All other feeling words describe either combinations or various intensities of these. To avoid the pitfalls involved with expressing emotions, complete the excrcises using only the basic feeling labels given in the next exercise.

If you can't feel angry when you need to assert yourself, the following exercises will help you:

• Replacing Misinformation about Anger

• Uses of Anger

• Replacing Unclear Labels

If you have difficulty experiencing the fear and anxiety that anger defends, or if you tend to blame outside sources for either your anger or your fear, the following exercises will be helpful:

• Replacing Misinformation about Anger

• Taking Responsibility

• Owning the Fear

Each Emotion Has a Purpose

You may have been brought up in a home where many taboos controlled emotions and their expression. If so, you have been taught that it's not okay to feel. If feelings were unacceptable, you had no need to learn what a feeling is or how to label it. This situation makes it very difficult to experience, use, and communicate feelings in a productive way.

The first step in overcoming your experience is to re-educate yourself by proving that the taboos which imply the "badness" of a feeling are false beliefs. On the contrary, every feeling is good. Each has a specific purpose that enhances your ability to cope with life, as well as to ensure the survival of the human race.

Below is a list of six feelings. Write what you think is the function of each.

Sadness _____

Loneliness _____

Guilt _____

Inadequacy _____

Fear _____

Gladness _____

Review each of these emotions and your answer. Then, ask yourself: What would life really be like without this feeling?

Feeling the Emotion

Many people mislabel the feeling experience by applying one label to most of their physiological sensations. They then behave according to that label. In order to express your feelings clearly, you need to distinguish the various sensations and name them accurately.

The following exercise requires that you be relaxed. Go to a quiet place. Get comfortable. Play the tape or deep breathe to the count of three until you are relaxed and your mind is clear.

Do only one or two of these visualizations at each sitting. Make sure that you relax and clear your mind after each one. It is best to end each sitting by visualizing *gladness.*

As you follow the directions, note your body's physical reactions. These reactions *are* the feeling.

Gladness

Remember a moment of success. Go over the hard work, the labor involved in achieving this success. Then put yourself into the moment of completion—that point when you looked at the finished product and knew it was a job well done.

What were your thoughts? _____

_____

_____

_____

How is your body reacting? _____

_____

Remember when you thought, "This is the greatest moment of my life." Relive that moment as though it were a movie and you the star. See the people around you. Know the joy. Let yourself smile.

How does your body feel? _____

Take this feeling with you as you go on with your day.

Sadness

Visualize a small child whose pet has just died. In your mind, direct a movie about this child. See the surroundings. Hear the sounds. Think the child's thoughts.

What parts of your body experience this feeling? _____

_____

_____

Describe a similar experience from your life. _____

_____

_____

_____

Fear

Think of a time when you were frightened. It can be an enjoyable fear—a roller coaster ride or a scary movie, for example. Relive that experience. See it in your mind's eye. Think the thoughts. Remember all the details you can.

What does your body do during this replay? _____

_____

_____

Anger

Tighten your fists. Clench your teeth. Imagine you are walking through a department store. See the details of the store—the colors, the smells, the sounds. Ahead you see someone you care about, whose face you visualize clearly, being belittled by a stranger.

What do you think? _____

_____

_____

_____

What do you say? _____

_____

_____

_____

How does your body respond? _____

_____

_____

"Feeling Labels" and "Feeling Statements"

It is important to know how to express feelings verbally by choosing "feeling labels" and "feeling statements" that are clear and precise. Below is a guide that will help when you search for a word to describe a feeling and form a sentence to convey this information to another:

1. Become familiar with the basic feeling labels. These are listed below, followed by other labels that describe different nuances of the emotion:

   Afraid—nervous, scared, terrified

   Sad—unhappy, mournful

   Guilty—ashamed, remorseful

   Inadequate—embarrassed, humiliated

   Lonely—lonesome

   Angry—annoyed, irritated, irate, furious, enraged

   Glad—content, relieved, satisfied, happy, joyous

2. If you use the words "that" or "like" with the feeling label, you are expressing a thought or an opinion, not a feeling.

   EXAMPLE: I feel that you have done a good job.

   TRANSLATES TO: I think you have done a good job.

   Notice that this sentence offers no information about the internal physiological reaction.

3. If you can substitute the word "think" for the word "feel" in your feeling statement and it still makes sense, you are stating a thought, not a feeling.

   EXAMPLE: I feel he is making a mistake.

   TRANSLATES TO: I think he is making a mistake.

   This is a judgment, an interpretation of the external event, not a description of your internal response.

4. Feeling labels are adjectives that describe the physiological sensation within your body. Their purpose is to convey information about you. Therefore:

   A. Do not use an adjective to describe a situation in which more than one feeling is possible.

   EXAMPLE: I feel different (powerless, lost, hurt, dizzy, confused).

   One person may be happy to be different, another may be afraid, and another may be sad.

   B. Avoid using a verb as a feeling label. Verbs denote action, judgment, and blame.

   EXAMPLE: I feel cheated.

   This statement says that someone did something that you judge as cheating, and whatever physiological sensation you have is that person's fault. Other verbs commonly misused as feeling labels are: blamed, betrayed, abandoned, distanced, rejected, neglected, etc.

5. When you can substitute "am" for "feel" in your feeling statement, there is a high probability that you are describing a feeling.

   EXAMPLE: I *feel* happy. I *am* happy.

The Feeling Formula

If you want your feelings to be useful tools, take possession of them; own your perception that created them, and be careful not to blame either on others. A simple formula may help you:

>**I FEEL** *(feeling label)* **WHEN I** *(how you see the event).*

>**EXAMPLE:** I feel afraid when I speak in front of a crowd.

This formula may seem unnatural when you first use it. With practice it will become more familiar and more comfortable. You can practice by completing the statements below with events from your past.

I felt sad when I _____

_____

_____

I felt inadequate when I _____

_____

_____

I felt guilty when I _____

_____

_____

I felt afraid when I _____

_____

_____

I felt happy when I _____

_____

Repeat each statement out loud after you've filled in the blank area.

Practice in Stating Feelings

Below are two more exercises that you can do to familiarize yourself with feeling labels and feeling statements.

Watching an Old Movie

Watch a movie, preferably one you've already seen. Be aware of your body as you watch each scene. Put a feeling label on each sensation as it occurs by using the simple statement:

I FEEL _____

Nightly Review

At night, review the major events of your day. Remember how you felt in each situation. Using the formula, write feeling statements for each event. Although you can formulate the statements mentally, the written exercise is more effective.

Event _____

Feeling Statement _____

Event _____

Feeling Statement _____

Event _____

Feeling Statement _____

Event _____

Feeling Statement _____

Replacing Misinformation about Anger

If you have difficulty feeling anger, you need to begin by giving yourself permission. Try to replace misinformation with facts. The misconceptions about anger discussed in chapter 4 and their refuting truths are as follows:

- **Anger Is an Accusation; Anger Equals Disapproval.** Anger is an internal physiological reaction to an extenal event. The person who is angry is protecting self from a perceived threat. It has nothing to do with another's "rightness" or "wrongness."

- **Anger Is Dangerous.** Anger itself is not dangerous, harmful, or violent. Anger is internal. The way some people act out their anger may be dangerous. But these actions are behavior, not feeling.

- **Ladies Don't Get Angry.** I am sure there are many things a lady doesn't do. Feeling angry isn't one of them. All human beings, not just men, can benefit from anger.

- **Anger Is Bad.** Anger is neither good nor bad. It has a function. When used as intended, it is productive and useful.

- **Anger Is a Sin.** It is not a sin to feel angry. If you believe it is un-Christian to experience anger, read the New Testament again and think about Christ's emotional responses.

- **The Other Person Is Responsible.** Each person is responsible for his own feelings, including anger. No one can reach in and turn on the adrenaline switch for another. That switch is turned on by the person's own interpretation of the event.

Review "What Your Answers Show about Attitudes" in chapter 1. Are there any pieces of misinformation about anger that you discovered there that aren't discussed above? Was anger used in your upbringing as a device for punishment, control, attack, threat, manipulation, or other purposes? Whatever you witnessed then, you absorbed as the proper uses of anger. And that may be false information which impedes the productive use of anger.

Write the misinformation that you assimilated during your early life. Disprove each of these beliefs by writing information that you have learned from this book or elsewhere in your experience.

Misinformation _____

True Information _____

Misinformation _____

True Information _____

Misinformation _____

True Information _____

Misinformation _____

True Information _____

Misinformation _____

True Information _____

Misinformation _____

True Information _____

Uses of Anger

If you have trouble feeling anger, knowledge of its function and usefulness will help you solidify the idea that it's not only an acceptable emotion, but also a necessary one. If you don't have difficulty feeling anger, but you express it in a destructive way, understanding its uses can help you choose *how* and *when* to use it productively.

Below is a list of anger's functions. Review chapter 2 and write an example of ways you've used or seen anger being used in each of these functions. If you can't think of an example from personal experience, ask your friends for examples from their lives.

Survival _____

_____

Cultural _____

_____

Social Regulator _____

_____

Social Bonding/Social Change: _____

_____

Communication _____

_____

Motivation _____

_____

Psychological Protection _____

_____

Replacing Unclear Labels

Another helpful way to become used to the idea that you have angry feelings is to replace the unclear "feeling labels" that you use with the word "angry."

Review the examples of unclear labels that are presented in chapter 4. List below those that you often use; add to this list any unclear labels that you use which aren't listed in chapter 4. Then think of a time when you used this label. Replace it with the word "angry" and write out the sentence.

EXAMPLE:

UNCLEAR LABEL ___upset___ USE "ANGRY" ___I felt angry___
___when I thought you weren't listening to me.___

UNCLEAR LABEL _____ USE "ANGRY" _____

_____

UNCLEAR LABEL _____ USE "ANGRY" _____

_____

UNCLEAR LABEL _____ USE "ANGRY" _____

_____

UNCLEAR LABEL _____ USE "ANGRY" _____

_____

UNCLEAR LABEL _____ USE "ANGRY" _____

_____

Now say each sentence out loud. You don't have to feel it; just say it.

Go to a quiet place. Using a relaxation tape or breathing to the count of three, clear your mind. Relive the scene that involved the unclear label. As you visualize the scene, replace the unclear label with the word "angry."

Replacing Misinformation about Fear

If you think that you experience anger more often than others do, perhaps you are unable to recognize and label the fear and anxiety sensation that precedes anger. Misinformation could be keeping you from experiencing fear. Here are three common misconceptions about fear, followed by the truth:

- **Fear Is Bad.** Every feeling has a function. The human race wouldn't be here today, you would not be here today, if it weren't for fear. It is the physiological sensation that signals danger. It readies the body for action when threat is near. It is fear that slams on the brakes when you are driving sixty miles an hour down the highway and a car cuts you off. It is fear that saves your life.

- **Men Don't Feel Fear.** Fear, or the lack of it, has nothing to do with manhood. The real point is whether you use your fear in an intelligent way. Do you get out of situations where there is nothing to be won and you would be hurt by the fight? Do you stay to fight in situations that are important? Can you tell the difference? It is the choice of flight or fight. If you aren't able to experience fear, you are always stuck in the fight.

- **Fear Is the Lack of Courage.** It is not courageous to be devoid of fear. Courage is feeling fear and performing the necessary task anyway. If the task isn't necessary or meaningful to you, why risk it? Only fools and robots never feel afraid.

List the false lessons you were taught about fear during your early life. Remember that you learn not only from what is said, but from what people do or don't do. Then disprove each of these misconceptions by writing accurate information.

Misinformation _____

_____

True Information _____

_____

Misinformation _____

_____

True Information _____

_____

Misinformation _____

_____

True Information _____

_____

Misinformation _____

_____

True Information _____

_____

Review your life. Can you think of any conflict when you stayed to fight, either physically or verbally, that would have turned out better for you if you had backed off or left? Describe more than one incident.

_____

_____

_____

_____

_____

_____

Taking Responsibility

You cannot use anger productively until you stop blaming others for your angry feelings. The following type of sentence helps to do this:

I FEEL *(angry)* WHEN I THINK *(how you see the event).*

EXAMPLE: I feel angry when I think you are putting me down.

This statement presents two pieces of information about yourself. It tells the other person your interpretation of his behavior and your feeling reaction to that interpretation. It also provides the opportunity for him to let you know whether your interpretation is accurate. If it isn't, you don't need the anger. If it is, you need to use the anger to develop an assertive response.

This formula may seem unnatural when you first use it. With practice it will become more comfortable. To begin practicing it, write three examples of times you've felt angry. Then write your anger statement using the formula.

Situation _____

I felt angry when I thought _____

_____

_____

Situation _____

I felt angry when I thought _____

_____

_____

Situation _____

I felt angry when I thought _____

_____

_____

Repeat each statement of anger out loud after you've filled in the blank area.

Owning the Fear

Another feeling formula, which helps you take responsibility for your angry feelings, involves the fact that anger is a protective device that acts as a defense to hide fear. This formula is:

I FEEL *(angry)* WHEN I'M *(a label for fear)*.

EXAMPLE: I feel angry when I'm nervous.

This statement takes into account the fact that some type of fear and anxiety always underlies the anger. You acknowledge ownership of the fear sensation, as well as the angry feeling. If you practice enough, you will begin to experience the fear and anxiety before it turns to anger. You will then have choices: you can express the fear; leave the threatening situation; or move into anger and use it to assert self.

Think over the past three days. When have you felt angry? Make a list of these events.

ANGRY EVENT _____

ANGRY EVENT _____

ANGRY EVENT _____

ANGRY EVENT _____

Using a relaxation tape or breathing to the count of three, clear your mind and relax. Visualize each angry incident listed above. As you relive each incident, repeat the formula using the appropriate fear label: anxious, afraid, nervous, etc.

Thoughts

When you are making changes in thinking, it doesn't matter whether you have difficulty feeling anger or you seem to feel it too often. The core element in both situations is an image of your identity that denies your worthiness as a human being. Problems of thought that maintain a denying self-concept and thereby affect anger are misinterpretation of the event, inaccurate judgments of self and others, and excessive negative self-statements.

The following exercises, practiced on a regular, consistent basis, help to alleviate such problems:

• Reinterpreting the Event

• Daily Review

• Stopping the Judgments

• Judging Self More Accurately

• Judging Others More Accurately

• Developing Positive Self-Statements

Reinterpreting the Event

The greatest spur to excessive anger is misinterpretation of events: (1) you misunderstand what is being said or done; (2) you react to situations as though you were the center of attention, thereby taking everything very personally.

List three events that you responded to with anger. What was your interpretation? Remember *exactly* what was said or done that offended you. Write three other possible interpretations.

Event _____

_____

Interpretation _____

_____

Possible Interpretation _____

_____

Possible Interpretation _____

_____

Possible Interpretation _____

_____

Event _____

_____

Interpretation _____

_____

Possible Interpretation _____

_____

Possible Interpretation _____

_____

Possible Interpretation _____

_____

Event _____

_____

Interpretation _____

_____

Possible Interpretation _____

_____

Possible Interpretation _____

_____

Possible Interpretation _____

_____

Daily Review

If you are like most human beings, you tend to replay angry incidents over and over in your mind. In doing so, you continue to use the original assessment of the situation. If that assessment was inaccurate, you are reinforcing a misinterpretation. Future interactions with the people involved or future similar experiences will reactivate the misinterpretation, influencing your emotional and behavioral responses. In order to step out of this destructive circle, evaluate the accuracy of your interpretations as soon as possible.

Before retiring for the evening, review your day. When did you feel angry? How did you interpret what was said or done? What are three other interpretations of the event? Did you take what was said personally, when it wasn't meant that way?

If you can't think of other interpretations, then either your interpretation is accurate and you need to take positive action to assert self, or your interpretation is inaccurate and you need assistance in reinterpreting the event. One way to obtain this assistance is to ask a friend for possible interpretations. Another way is to approach the other person involved in the angry incident. In a nonaccusatory manner, explain your understanding of what was said or done and ask whether that meaning was intended.

Write down your review using the format below. Do this exercise daily until you discover yourself doing it automatically when you feel angry.

Event _____

_____

Interpretation _____

_____

Possible Interpretation _____

_____

Possible Interpretation _____

_____

Possible Interpretation _____

_____

Event _____

_____

Interpretation _____

_____

Possible Interpretation _____

_____

Possible Interpretation _____

_____

Possible Interpretation _____

_____

Event _____

_____

Interpretation _____

_____

Possible Interpretation _____

_____

Possible Interpretation _____

_____

Look over the possible interpretations for each event. Decide which seems most accurate.

Now go to a quiet place. Relax and clear your mind by using a relaxation tape or by breathing to the count of three. Visualize each event. Apply the new interpretation and notice how you respond.

Stopping the Judgments

Often harsh, punitive, angry feelings are continually heightened by inaccurate judgments. These judgments tend to dehumanize the person at whom they are aimed. They make her into an object of scorn, something worthy of attack or insult. Self or others may be the target of these judgments. When you remove them from your thoughts, the intensity of your anger diminishes, and you find it difficult to use your anger destructively.

How you evaluate yourself after you make a mistake is often an inaccurate, overly harsh judgment. For instance, after I make a mistake, I mentally hear myself saying, "Damn it. I can't do anything right." This judgment is inaccurate. I do many things right. It just happens I erred on this one. Other self-judgments that people have shared with me are, "I'm stupid," "I'm a jerk," "I'm no good."

Inaccurate judgments about others also heighten and regenerate anger. Remember times when you have been angry with someone. What "names" did you call that person? These "names" could be thoughts or actual verbalizations. In either case, they are usually judgments that are extreme and dehumanizing. One of my personal favorites, when a colleague makes a mistake that affects me, is mentally to call him an "idiot." This denunciation is inaccurate. I know that he is a highly intelligent man who, in this particular instance, happens to have made a mistake.

Judging Self More Accurately

List the judgments you make about yourself after you make a mistake. Then disprove each of these with an accurate statement.

Judgment _____

This is wrong because _____

_____

Judgment _____

This is wrong because _____

_____

Judgment _____

This is wrong because _____

_____

Now, say each judgment out loud, followed by the word **STOP,** three times.

> **EXAMPLE:** I can't do anything right—**STOP.**

Say this sentence again three times, adding the reason the judgment is incorrect.

> **EXAMPLE:** I can't do anything right—**STOP**—That's wrong, I do many things right.

As you go through your day, listen for the inaccurate judgments you make about yourself. Use this technique to replace these false, hurtful judgments with more truthful, gentler ones.

Judging Others More Accurately

What are the most common judgments you make about others? List these below and then disprove each by using a more accurate statement.

Judgment _____

This is incorrect because _____

_____

Judgment _____

This is incorrect because _____

_____

Judgment _____

This is incorrect because _____

_____

Now, say each judgment out loud, followed by the word **STOP,** three times.

> **EXAMPLE:** He's an idiot—**STOP.**

Say the judgment again three times, adding why it is incorrect.

> **EXAMPLE:** He's an idiot—**STOP**—That's incorrect, he's a highly intelligent man who made a mistake.

As you go through your day, listen for the inaccurate judgments that you make about others. Use this technique to replace these incorrect, hurtful judgments with more accurate, gentler ones.

Developing Positive Self-Statements

An affirming self-concept exists when your positive statements about yourself outnumber negative ones. When a thought is imprinted on the brain, it remains there forever. It can be removed only by trauma or organic deterioration. Your mind is not like a tape recorder; the negative evaluations that you have internalized about yourself cannot be taken out, erased, or printed over.

The only way to change a denying self-concept to an affirming one is to increase the number of positive self-statements so that they dominate the negative ones. This technique is most effective when the new statements counteract the negative evaluations.

To discover your strongest negative self-statements, remember the times you were punished or reprimanded as a child. What was said to you? How did you personalize these events as evaluations of self? If nothing was said to you—for instance, you were sent to your room or ignored—how did you evaluate yourself? Because these evaluations do not describe what you did, but who you are as a human being, they aren't true. You are not a bad person because you didn't clean your room, or you forgot to take the garbage out, or you received a poor grade, or you fought with your sister. I don't even know for sure that these behaviors are bad; I do know that you are not. Unfortunately, it is not enough for me to know this fact. You need to believe it.

List three of the negative things you say about yourself. Then for each, indicate three things that you have done which show that the insult is unjust.

Negative Self-Statement _____

_____

This is incorrect because I've _____

_____

_____

Negative Self-Statement _____

_____

This is incorrect because I've _____

_____

_____

Negative Self-Statement _____

_____

This is incorrect because I've _____

_____

_____

Again, list the three negative self-statements from above. Think of an accurate, positive self-statement that counteracts it.

Negative Self-Statement _____

_____

Positive Self-Statement _____

_____

Negative Self-Statement _____

_____

Positive Self-Statement _____

_____

Negative Self-Statement _____

_____

Positive Self-Statement _____

_____

Go to a quiet place. Relax and clear your mind by using a relaxation tape or breathing to the count of three. The more relaxed you are, the more effective this exercise will be.

When you are relaxed, repeat each positive statement five times.

Behaviors

There are two types of assertive behaviors. The first is an immediate event, which occurs at the moment your self-esteem is threatened. The second is a series of actions you undertake to alleviate situations that are a constant assault on your image of self as a person worthy of respect. Both acts require you to recognize your anger and then assert self without harming yourself or someone else.

If you tend to turn anger inward and have difficulty expressing it, the following exercises will be helpful:

• "I'm Angry" Is Okay

• Saying "I'm Angry" Is Okay

If the way you express anger is basically aggressive, the following exercises will help you become more assertive:

• Reducing the Anger Arousal

• Options Other Than Aggression

• Interrupting an Aggressive Response

One last exercise helps you plan an assertive process:

• Taking Action

"I'm Angry" Is Okay

If you are more likely to berate yourself than to blame others, you may need to begin by giving yourself permission to say the labels that indicate anger. Do the exercise "Replacing Unclear Labels" (p. 66) in the section of this chapter about emotions.

Behaviors that indicate unfelt anger are self-pity, "why" questions, and action verbs used as feeling labels.

Review your day. When did you feel sorry for yourself? Ask yourself what you were angry about. Did you use any "why" questions that did not seek information? Write them out as feeling statements. Did you use verbs, such as "cheated," "trapped," or "rejected," as if they were your feelings? Use the format described in the exercise "Taking Responsibility" (p. 69) to write them down as anger.

Self-Pity _____

_____

Object of Anger _____

_____

"Why" Questions _____

_____

_____

Anger Statements _____

_____

_____

Verbs as Feelings _____

Expressed as Anger _____

Expressed as Anger _____

Saying "I'm Angry" Is Okay

Review the behaviors you have listed that indicate you may be angry. Now go to a quiet place. Relax and clear your mind by using a relaxation tape or breathing to the count of three.

Replay each incident separately, replacing the nonassertive behavior with the statement about your anger. Play the scene through to the end. When you have finished replaying all the incidents, ask yourself the following questions:

• Was the outcome what you feared would happen if you expressed your anger?

• How did others react in your new scenario?

• How did you feel about yourself afterwards?

Tomorrow, as you go through your day, be aware of your behaviors that indicate anger. When one occurs with someone you trust, use an assertive statement to tell him that you feel angry. You don't have to shout your anger. You don't have to look angry. Just say the words:

I feel angry when I think _____

Remember, you will merely be presenting information about yourself to that person. Therefore, you don't have to explain your feeling, justify it, or defend it. Don't be drawn into an argument. My response to someone who attempts to draw me into an argument is, "I just wanted you to know how I was feeling."

Reducing the Anger Arousal

Some people have told me that they deal with their aggressive tendencies by doing some physical activity to reduce the anger before they use it destructively. Exercise lowers the adrenaline that causes the sensation of anger, but it does not change the thoughts that produced the adrenaline. When these thoughts return, so does the anger and the possibility of aggression.

If you have used physical activity to reduce your anger, I recommend that you continue. Or if you think this approach may work for you, give it a try.

After the level of adrenaline and anger drops, review the exercises in the thought section of this chapter. This strategy will help to change unrealistic perceptions of threats, and you may discover yourself requiring less physical activity.

Options Other Than Aggression

It is perfectly healthy and normal to feel angry. It is not helpful to you or to other people when you use that anger to do harm. The problem is not that you feel anger; what matters is what you do with it. To change an aggressive response, you need to interrupt the process before you attack.

Each evening, review your day. When did you have an aggressive episode, a situation in which you felt angry and acted destructively? Which option would have been most comfortable for you to use when you felt your anger begin?

I feel angry when I think _____

or

I'm feeling too angry to discuss this. I'll get back to you when I've given it some thought.
Then complete the following:

Aggressive Episode _____

Option _____

_____

Aggressive Episode _____

Option _____

_____

Aggressive Episode _____

Option _____

_____

Interrupting an Aggressive Response

Go to a quiet place. Relax and clear your mind by using a relaxation tape or breathing to the count of three. Review the aggressive episodes you listed. Try to remember the point at which you began feeling angry. Replay the first episode and, when you arrive at that point, think **"STOP."**

Now continue to imagine the episode using the option you chose. Repeat this procedure for all the aggressive episodes you wrote down. When you finish, ask yourself the following questions:

• How did others react to my new option?

• How did I feel about myself afterwards?

Tomorrow, as you go through your day, be aware of the point when your anger starts. Then, just once, when you feel the anger begin, think "**STOP**." Say the option you feel most comfortable using.

Tomorrow evening, as you review your day, ask yourself:

• How did others react to my "new" expression of anger?

• How did I feel about myself afterwards?

• How does this feeling compare to the feelings you have after hurting someone with your anger?

Taking Action

If you are in a situation in which you are constantly unhappy or angry, now may be the time for change. The responsibility for your happiness or your anger is yours. The person responsible for change is therefore you.

Before answering the questions below, review the passages about behavior in chapters 3 and 4.

What is the problem that elicits your emotional response? Be specific.

_____

_____

What do you need, and what can you do to get it?

_____

_____

What is your plan for changing your situation? Write specific details. Outline your plan step by step. Indicate a starting date for each step.

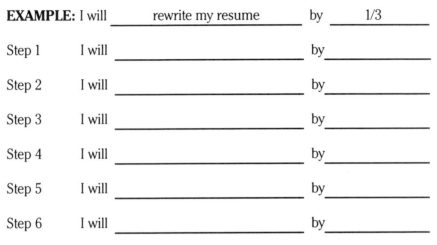

EXAMPLE: I will _____rewrite my resume_____ by _____1/3_____

Step 1   I will _____ by_____

Step 2   I will _____ by_____

Step 3   I will _____ by_____

Step 4   I will _____ by_____

Step 5   I will _____ by_____

Step 6   I will _____ by_____

As you begin working through these exercises and practicing them in your daily activities, people will respond differently to you. Some won't know how to react and will avoid you. This reaction may disturb you. On the other hand, as you use your angry feelings to assert self, and your anger becomes less hurtful, others will want to spend more time with you. Over time you will discover that these relationships become deeper and stronger.

As people decide whether to be with the new you, you too will also choose your own companions. Your decisions may lead you away from people you formerly sought and toward those you previously wouldn't have chosen. You will realize that friends who batter your self-esteem with put-downs and sarcasm hold you back. You may develop an aversion to them. Those who tend to enhance your self-esteem by honest support and positive feedback are those who attract you.

CHAPTER SIX

Responding to Another Person's Anger

My husband yells about the bills; my girlfriend gets angry and avoids me; my boss goes into a tirade about things that are beyond my control; my coworker talks about me behind my back and thinks I don't know it. Clients have made these statements and a multitude of others and then asked me how they should deal with the other person's anger. I routinely answer, "As an adult." This reply may seem simple, even flippant; it is neither.

The greatest problem in encountering another's anger is that people return to a child's perspective of powerlessness and vulnerability and react on childhood misinformation. For instance, you don't have to "deal" with any other person's anger. The angry feeling is his. It's his adrenaline. Therefore, it is his responsibility to deal with it. In fact, he is the only person who can deal with it. Your responsibility is merely to respond in a way that you hope will open the door to greater trust and intimacy. The more you know about anger and the more work you've done concerning your own angry feelings, the easier your role will be. Therefore, make sure you've completed the preceding five chapters before you attempt this one. If you put forth some effort and follow four basic guidelines, you will be able to respond effectively to another person's anger.

If you suspect that the person's anger will be expressed violently—get away!

No one has the right to strike or harm you. You are not anyone's punching bag. You are a human being. As a human being, you do not have to remain in a place, or near a person, where danger is an imminent possibility. Leave!

Get away from the source of potential harm!

There are no exceptions to this guideline. If you are in a situation in which you have been physically assaulted, seek professional advice. There are counselors and groups at shelters, mental health clinics, and social service departments whose main purpose is to assist people who are in potentially violent situations. Understand several facts:

• You did not cause the violent behavior.

• The behavior will not automatically stop.

• You have the right to seek assistance.

Understand and attempt to use your own anger productively.

As long as you believe the misinformation about anger that you have carried since childhood, and as long as your own anger causes you intense discomfort, you won't be able to respond effectively to other people's angry feelings. You won't be able to listen properly to the person's message, or to respond assertively if she expresses her anger aggressively. I therefore recommend that you review the informational areas and the exercises in this manual again to be sure that you have attained enough understanding and comfort with your own anger to be effective when you respond to another's.

Assert self when verbally attacked.

If the first guideline is satisfied and you don't think you are in danger of physical harm, stand firm against any verbal put-downs. The well-being of your self-concept is integral to your physical, as well as your emotional health. Protect it. Be assertive without being aggressive.

Everyone has the right to feel angry, but they do not have the right to use that anger to hurt others. I use three basic responses when friends, co-workers, or intimates express their anger in the form of verbal attack: "I'm willing to listen to you as long as you stop the attack"; "I want to hear what you're angry about, and I can't while you put me down"; or, a more adamant response, "You don't have the right to attack me that way. If you want me to listen, stop the put-downs."

Neither you nor I can make a person stop a verbal attack. If you've used an assertive statement and the individual continues put-downs, your role is to assert self. You may excuse yourself and leave. As an alternative, you can ask the other person to leave. If the attacks are ongoing, you begin the assertive process necessary to change your situation. In any of these scenarios, you have made it possible for your affirming self-concept to remain intact.

Respond as one adult human being to another.

After you have observed the first three guidelines, your own expectations may still obstruct your responding in a productive way when someone else is angry. These expectations you learned in childhood, when you were vulnerable and relatively powerless. Review the questions, "What Are Your Expectations?" and "How Did You Respond?" in chapter 1. What you find there reveals how you have been conditioned to respond. If your conditioning includes the expectation of harm, accusation, or punishment, you probably defend against or ward off an attack, even if you are not being attacked. You interpret the anger through the distorting glass of your childhood experience. That interpretation produces a child's response, modified for an adult's use. (Review your answers to the question "How Do You Respond to Anger?" in chapter 1.) If you are intent on preparing your defense, you can't accurately hear what the angry person is saying to you. You miss the "now." Because your interpretation of the present is based on your history rather than on what is actually being said, your response can't help but be ineffective.

Therefore, the first objective in responding to someone's anger is movement beyond old expectations and interpretations. That goal accomplished, you are in a better position to hear what others say to you. You may make this change in two steps: interrupt your old expectations with a "now" statement, and command yourself to listen. Anger is a form of communication. What is the person trying to tell you? Does she see self as trapped, cheated, treated unfairly? The only way to find out is to **LISTEN.**

For example, if you expect anger to be punishing and a friend expresses angry feelings, you can slow down your reactions by practicing several strategies:

1. As you begin to tense, think **"STOP!"**

2. Take a breath, hold it to the count of three, and let it out slowly.

3. Mentally negate the expectation with a "now" statement such as, "This person can't punish me. He is a peer."

4. Tell yourself to listen. "I'll just listen to hear what he's angry about."

The next objective is to reply to your friend's message. Speak specifically to what you heard him say. Do not generalize with such answers as "I know how you feel," or "I understand your anger." These statements sound condescending and empty. Let your friend hear back in your own words what you heard him say to you.

Suppose you think your friend is saying that he thinks you cheated him. Maybe at the beginning of the summer you had sold him a boat and a week later the motor gave out. He had to replace it. Make sure you are hearing him clearly by asking, "Are you telling me that you think I've cheated you?" If the answer is no, ask for further clarification. Let him know you are trying to understand. If the answer is yes, ask for specific details about his accusation. Ask if he believes that you sold him the boat knowing that the motor was about to break.

After listening to the details, your next response demands a deep level of honesty. If he is right, and you did cheat him, tell him the truth; ask whether together you can develop a means of replacing the motor that is fair to both of you. This honesty and compromise may seem difficult, but it is the way mature, responsible adults behave. They take responsibility for their actions. They don't deny, lie, or hide from their mistakes. Children who are afraid of severe punishment from their more powerful parents have a need for these clandestine behaviors, but mature adults do not. Such subterfuge only adds to a denying self-concept.

If you did not cheat your friend, if you did not know about the deficiencies in the motor, present the facts. When the facts are real, you need not argue them or defend them. They can stand on their own. There is nothing you can do if your friend won't accept them. Just present the facts and let him decide for himself whether to persist in thinking you cheated. You have done your part. The rest is up to him. It is his interpretation of events. It is his anger.

Interrupting Expectations

The most important part of an effective reply when someone confronts you in anger is listening for a clear, undistorted message. Learned expectations interfere with your ability to hear what is actually said. You can interrupt your conditioned expectations with appropriate "now" statements.

List three situations in which someone else expressed anger. Which of your expectations from the questions "What Are Your Expectations?" and "How Did You Respond?" in chapter 1 came to mind? What is an appropriate "now" statement that negates the old expectation? (A "now" statement shows how the specific expectation is false because of your present status as an adult.)

EXAMPLE: I won't be spanked. I am his equal.

Situation _____

Expectation _____

"Now" Statement _____

Situation _____

Expectation _____

"Now" Statement _____

Situation _____

Expectation _____

"Now" Statement _____

Go to a quiet place. Relax and clear your mind by using a relaxation tape or breathing to the count of three. Replay the angry situation in your mind.

When you begin to feel tense, think **"STOP!"**

Take a deep breath, count to three, and slowly let it out.
Think the "now" statement.
Do this same procedure for each situation that you listed.

Listening and Clarifying

Anger carries a message about the person who is angry. If you keep this function in mind, you will be able to listen more easily to another's anger.

Think of situations in which you were talking with someone who felt angry. What did she say? What was her message, her understanding of the events that incited her anger? What would your clarifying response be in each case? A clarifying response begins, "Are you saying that ... ?" or "Do you think ... ?" If you have no idea of what her message is, your reply shows her that you are trying to understand and are asking her to tell you again what the anger is about.

Situation _____

_____

He/She Thinks _____

_____

Clarifying Response _____

_____

Situation _____

_____

He/She Thinks _____

_____

Clarifying Response _____

_____

Situation _____

_____

He/She Thinks _____

_____

Clarifying Response _____ _____

_____

Emotions were never meant to be destructive or harmful. In fact, the opposite is true. An emotion is a physiological sensation, the same as hunger. Like
hunger, which signals the need for nourishment, each feeling functions to
satisfy or warn of a human need. For this reason, feelings cannot be classified
as "good" or "bad," "positive" or "negative." They are merely utilitarian. It is
therefore counterproductive to curb or control emotions, release them, re-
solve them, or ventilate them. Instead, it is necessary to recognize each feeling, understand its function, and then choose a behavior that responds to that
function.

Human beings do not have to learn, but are naturally constituted to
experience emotions. They must learn what each feeling is and its possible
functions. Then, to obtain the desired effects, they must learn the most productive ways of expressing and reacting to that feeling. When these learning
processes are interrupted, carried out inadequately, or totally ignored in a
person's life, the results are ineffective, at the least, and at worst, extremely
harmful. On the other hand, when taught well, emotions are tools for effective living.

Anger is no exception. With the deadline for this book pressing closer,
I wanted to take a day off from my job and write. Having a good working
relationship with my boss, I called her at home and asked, "If I don't come in
today, will you be terribly angry?" She said "Yes." My next question to her
was, "Will I live through the consequences of that and have a job?" She replied, "Yes." I took the day off. It was not her angry feeling that worried me,
but the behavior that she might use to express that anger had me on edge.
That principle applies to anyone's anger. It is not the emotion that is destructive, but the way a person expresses it.

Since my boss is not a vindictive person, my anxiety over a lost job
had little to do with her and much more to do with me—my fears and my
learned expectations. Once I could put those to rest with more accurate in-

formation, I was free to make a decision based on my priorities and not on potential, irrational interpretations. If she had said, "Yes, you will lose your job," I would have had a valid perception of reality. And that valuable piece of information would have become a strong variable in my decision. I probably would have gone to work.

You may be thinking, "You're lucky. You have a decent boss. Mine's a jerk." Luck had very little to do with it. Anger was much more important. The master's degree that I sought in 1982 because of angry feelings toward a supervisor opened up a world of options. I can now choose whether or not to work for a jerk.

When a person can recognize and understand her own anger, it becomes like a friend, a part of her life that brings enrichment. This relationship with her own anger enables her to stop being intimidated by other people's anger. These two results provide her with the freedom to make her own choices and the incentive to act on those choices.

Notes

CHAPTER TWO Taking a New Perspective on Anger

1. Edmund Jacobson, *Biology of Emotions* (Springfield, Ill.: Charles C. Thomas, 1967), presents a more detailed explanation of the physiology of emotions.

2. Norma D. Feshback and Kiki Roe, "Empathy in Six- and Seven-Year-Olds," *Child Development* 39 (1968): 133-45, used the four feeling themes of happiness, sadness, fear, and anger to measure conditions that encourage empathy.

3. Harvey A. Hornstein, *Cruelty and Kindness: A New Look at Aggression and Altruism* (Englewood Cliffs, N.J.: Prentice-Hall, 1976), 13-31, describes research studies he conducted that revolve around boundaries established by "we" vs. "they" attitudes. Not only do these attitudes lead to bonding for the "we" group, but they also heighten aggression toward group members of the "they" group. The way to lower aggression is to create social situations that increase the bonding of "we" and lower the boundaries established by a "they" perspective.

4. Albert Rothenberg, "On Anger," *American Journal of Psychiatry* 128 (October 1971): 458.

CHAPTER THREE Acknowledging the Complexities of Anger

1. David N. Daniels, Marshall F. Gilula, and Frank M. Ochberg, eds., *Violence and the Struggle for Existence* (Boston: Little, Brown, 1970), provides a more complete account of the many various theories about aggression.

2. John R. Marshall, "The Expression of Feelings," *Archives of General Psychiatry* 27 (December 1972): 786-90, reviews studies involving the free expression of feelings. He concludes that evidence supporting the therapy models of ventilation is inconclusive. In addition, research findings that treat aggression specifically raise strong doubts about the usefulness of ventilation as a means of reducing aggressive behavior.
    Murray Straus, "Leveling, Civility, and Violence in the Family," *Journal of Marriage and the Family* 36 (February 1974): 18, conducted a study of 385 couples to test the hypothesis that verbal expression of aggressive feelings lowers physical aggression. He found the opposite: "As the level of verbal aggression increases, the level of physical aggression increases dramatically."

3. Michael Kahn, "The Physiology of Catharsis," *Journal of Personality and Social Psychology* 3 (1966): 278-86, is a study of thirty-six male freshmen, aroused to a state of anger and assigned catharsis or noncatharsis conditions. The subjects' automatic responses were then measured for a twenty-minute recovery period. Catharsis did not lower the physiological arousal of anger.

4. Marshall, "The Expression of Feelings," 788.

5. Rothenberg, "On Anger," 458.

6. Ernest Becker, "Anthropological Notes on the Concept of Aggression," *Psychiatry* 25 (1962): 328-38, and Raymond W. Novaco, "The Functions and Regulation of the Arousal of Anger," *American Journal of Psychiatry* 133 (October 1976): 1124-27, contend that anger protects integrity and self-esteem, a concept that is integral to the model presented in this guide.

Loren Pankratz, Philip Levendusky, and Vincent Glaudin, "The Antecedents of Anger in a Sample of College Students," *Journal of Psychology* 92 (March 1976): 173-78.

7. Rothenberg, "On Anger," 458-59.

Hossain B. Danesh, "Anger and Fear," *American Journal of Psychiatry* 134 (October 1977): 1109-12, explores the connection between fear and anxiety, and anger.

8. Robert A. Green and Edward J. Murray, "Instigation to Aggression as a Function of Self-disclosure and Threat to Self-esteem," *Journal of Consulting and Clinical Psychology* 40 (1973): 440-43, found that, after self-disclosure a person is most vulnerable and self-esteem more easily threatened.

9. David C. Rimm, et al., "Group-Assertive Training in Treatment of Expression of Inappropriate Anger," *Psychological Reports* 34 (1974): 791-98, divided male volunteers who reported a history of aggression into a group trained in assertiveness and a placebo group. Those who received training showed significantly greater improvement in handling anger productively than the placebo group.

10. Danesh, "Anger and Fear," explores the three stages of fear and anger and the patterns these emotions take as protective mechanisms.

11. Danesh, "Anger and Fear," 1111.

Pankratz, Levendusky, and Glaudin, "The Antecedents of Anger."

CHAPTER FOUR Understanding How Anger Goes Awry

1. Arnold H. Buss, "Physical Aggression in Relation to Different Frustrations," *Journal of Abnormal and Social Psychology* 67 (1983): 1-7, explores the well-known connection between frustration and aggression by investigating three kinds of frustration and the impact each has on college students' aggression. He contends that the likely influence of the aggressive behavior is a greater determiner of aggression than the type of frustration.

Simply put, if a person thinks aggression will overcome an obstacle, he is more likely to act aggressively.

2. Albert Bandura, Dorothea Ross, and Sheila A. Ross, "Imitation of Film-Mediated Aggressive Models," *Journal of Abnormal and Social Psychology* 66 (1963): 3-11, demonstrate that aggression is learned, not only by imitating live role-models, but also by imitating actors on television and in movies.

3. Albert Bandura, *Aggression: A Social Learning Analysis* (Englewood Cliffs, N.J.: Prentice-Hall, 1973), presents a thorough explanation of the "social learning theory" concept that aggression is culturally permitted and mediated.

Carol Tavris, *Anger: The Misunderstood Emotion* (New York: Simon & Schuster, 1982), describes various cultural rites concerning anger and aggression.

4. Buss, "Physical Aggression," 2.

5. Rothenberg, "On Anger," 460.

6. Novaco, "The Functions and Regulation of the Arousal of Anger," 1125, discusses the defense of ego as a function of anger: "Anger externalizes the conflict by directing attention to something that is nonself...."

7. Rothenberg, "On Anger," 459. Not only do people remember experiences of threat, anxiety, and anger, but Dr. Rothenberg also contends that these memories influence people's perception throughout life. They engender a predisposition to anxiety and anger in relation to situations and persons.

8. Damaris J. Rohsenow and Ronald E. Smith, "Irrational Beliefs as Predictors of Negative Affective States," *Motivation and Emotion* 6 (1982): 299-314.

9. Rohsenow and Smith, "Irrational Beliefs," 306-311.

10. Raymond W. Novaco, "Stress Inoculation: A Cognitive Therapy for Anger and Its Application to a Case of Depression," *Journal of Consulting and Clinical Psychology* 47 (1977): 600-608.

11. Danesh, "Anger and Fear," 1111·1112, links the two feelings.
    Novaco, "Stress Inoculation," 601-607, links anger and depression.

12. Rothenberg, "On Anger," 456-57.

13. Christopher A. Innes, "Drug Use and Crime," *Bureau of Justice Statistics* (Washington, D.C.: Government Printing Office, July 1988), conducted this survey in 1986.

14. Feshback and Roe, "Empathy in Six- and Seven-Year-Olds," discovered that a significant number of boys have difficulty labeling fear.

15. Claudeen Cline-Naffziger, "Women's Lives and Frustration, Oppression and Anger: Some Alternatives," *Journal of Counseling Psychology* 21 (January 1974): 51-56, and Harriet E. Lerner, "Internal Prohibitions Against Female Anger," *American Journal of Psychoanalysis* 40 (1980): 137-48, both recognize this idea.

16. Stuart R. Garrison and Arnold Stolberg, "Modification of Anger in Children by Affective Imagery Training," *Journal of Abnormal Child Psychology* 11 (1983): 115-30, discuss the phenomenon of mislabeling aroused states. They explain that anger may be used by some people as a label for all physiological responses. Although their study is about children, I believe that it generalizes to adults.

CHAPTER FIVE Changing Your Experience of Anger

1. I have been a counselor since 1977 and a workshop presenter since 1982. In these roles, I have worked with many professionals who willingly shared their skills, techniques, and therapeutic exercises. I am sure that pieces of their work are in the exercises presented in this chapter.
    Throughout my professional life, I have listened to lectures on counseling techniques and approaches and read a multitude of journal articles and books. All of this input influenced the way I try to assist people's quest for effective ways to use anger. Below are the studies that I remember had the greatest impact on developing the presented exercises:
    Stuart R. Garrison and Arnold Stolberg, "Modification of Anger in Children by Affective Imagery Training," *Journal of Abnormal Child Psychology* 11 (1983): 115-30.
    Donald H. Meichenbaum and Joseph Goodman, "Training Impulsive Children to Talk to Themselves: A Means of Developing Self-contol," *Journal of Abnormal Psychology* 77 (1971): 115-26.
    Raymond W. Novaco, "Stress Inoculation: A Cognitive Therapy for Anger and Its Application to a Case of Depression," *Journal of Consulting and Clinical Psychology* 47 (1977): 600-608.

Paul W. Kettlewell and Donald F. Kausch, "The Generalization of the Effects of a Cognitive-Behavioral Treatment Program for Aggressive Children," *Journal of Abnormal Child Psychology* 11 (1983): 101-14.

James G. Hollandsworth, "Differentiating Assertion and Aggression: Some Behavioral Guidelines," *Behavior Therapy* 8 (1977): 347-52.

David C. Rimm, et al., "Group-Assertive Training in Treatment of Expression of Inappropriate Anger," *Psychological Reports* 34 (1974): 791-98.

Merna Dee Galassi and John P. Galassi, "Modifying Assertive and Aggressive Behavior Through Assertion Training," *Journal of College Student Personnel* 19 (September 1978): 453-56.

Harriet Goldhor Lerner, *The Dance of Anger* (New York: Harper & Row, 1985). When people ask, "What book can I read that will help me with my anger?," I recommend this one. Although it specifically speaks to women, I find most of the material appropriate to men also.

Bibliography

Bandura, Albert. *Aggression: A Social Learning Analysis.* Englewood Cliffs, N.J.: Prentice-Hall, 1973.

Bandura, Albert, Dorothea Ross, and Sheila A. Ross. "Imitation of Film-Mediated Aggressive Models." *Journal of Abnormal and Social Psychology* 66 (1963): 3-11.

Becker, Ernest. "Anthropological Notes on the Concept of Aggression." *Psychiatry* 25 (1962): 328-38.

Buss, Arnold H. "Physical Aggression in Relation to Different Frustrations." *Journal of Abnormal and Social Psychology* 67 (1983): 1-7.

Cline-Naffziger, Claudeen. "Women's Lives and Frustration, Oppression and Anger: Some Alternatives." *Journal of Counseling Psychology* 21 (January 1974): 51-56.

Danesh, Hossain B. "Anger and Fear." *American Journal of Psychiatry* 134 (October 1977): 1109-12.

Daniels, David N., Marshall F. Gilula, and Frank M. Ochberg, eds. *Violence and the Struggle for Existence.* Boston: Little, Brown, 1970.

Feshback, Norma D., and Kiki Roe. "Empathy in Six- and Seven-Year-Olds." *Child Development* 39 (1968): 133-45.

Galassi, Merna Dee, and John P. Galassi. "Modifying Assertive and Aggressive Behavior Through Assertion Training." *Journal of College Student Personnel* 19 (September 1978): 453-56.

Garrison, Stuart R., and Arnold Stolberg. "Modification of Anger in Children by Affective Imagery Training." *Journal of Abnormal Child Psychology* 11 (1983): 115-30.

Green, Robert A., and Edward J. Murray. "Instigation to Aggression as a Function of Self-disclosure and Threat to Self-esteem." *Journal of Consulting and Clinical Psychology* 40 (1973): 440-43.

Hollandsworth, James G. "Differentiating Assertion and Aggression: Some Behavioral Guidelines." *Behavior Therapy* 8 (1977): 347-52.

Hornstein, Harvey A. *Cruelty and Kindness: A New Look at Aggression and Altruism.* Englewood Cliffs, N.J.: Prentice-Hall, 1976.

Innes, Christopher A. "Drug Use and Crime." *Bureau of Justice Statistics,* Washington, D.C.: Government Printing Office, July 1988.

Jacobson, Edmund. *Biology of Emotions.* Springfield, Ill.: Charles C. Thomas, 1967.

Kahn, Michael. "The Physiology of Catharsis." *Journal of Personality and Social Psychology* 3 (1966): 278-86.

Kettlewell, Paul W., and Donald F. Kausch. "The Generalization of the Effects of a Cognitive-Behavioral Treatment Program for Aggressive Children." *Journal of Abnormal Child Psychology* 11 (1983): 101-14.

Lerner, Harriet E. "Internal Prohibitions Against Female Anger." *American Journal of Psychoanalysis* 40 (1980): 137-48.

Lerner, Harriet Goldhor. *The Dance of Anger*. New York: Harper & Row, 1985.

Marshall, John R. "The Expression of Feelings." *Archives of General Psychiatry* 27 (December 1972): 786-90.

Meichenbaum, Donald H., and Joseph Goodman. "Training Impulsive Children to Talk to Themselves: A Means of Developing Self- control." *Journal of Abnormal Psychology* 77 (1971): 115-26.

Novaco, Raymond W. "The Functions and Regulation of the Arousal of Anger." *American Journal of Psychiatry* 133 (October 1976): 1124-27.

_____ . "Stress Inoculation: A Cognitive Therapy for Anger and Its Application to a Case of Depression." *Journal of Consulting and Clinical Psychology* 45 (1977): 600-608.

Pankratz, Loren, Philip Levendusky, and Vincent Glaudin. "The Antecedents of Anger in a Sample of College Students." *Journal of Psychology* 92 (March 1976): 173-78.

Rimm, David C., et al. "Group-assertive Training in Treatment of Expression of Inappropriate Anger." *Psychological Reports* 34 (1974): 791-98.

Rohsenow, Damaris J., and Ronald E. Smith. "Irrational Beliefs as Predictors of Negative Affective States." *Motivation and Emotion* 6 (1982): 299-314.

Rothenberg, Albert. "On Anger." *American Journal of Psychiatry* 128 (October 1971): 454-60.

Straus, Murray. "Leveling, Civility, and Violence in the Family." *Journal of Marriage and the Family* 36 (February 1974): 13-29.

Tavris, Carol. *Anger: The Misunderstood Emotion*. New York: Simon & Schuster, 1982.

About the Author

Lorrainne Bilodeau is a Certified Addictions Counselor who trained at the Johnson Institute in Minneapolis and holds B.S. and M.S. degrees from Virginia Commonwealth University. She developed the "Encountering Anger" clinic, a seminar which she also facilitates, to help people learn to express and use their angry feelings. Human services organizations consulted her to develop anger management programs and to build teamwork within their agencies. In addition, she trained therapists to respond to clients' anger in healing ways.

Bilodeau established a program for clients who are prone to relapse and conducted a workshop about recovering persons of minority groups. A counselor for more than fifteen years, she developed "Stairway to Recovery: A Practical Guide to the 12 Steps," a video presentation to help recovering people understand the Twelve Steps philosophy of Alcoholics Anonymous.

Since 1987, Lorrainne Bilodeau has worked as program director and clinical director at chemical dependency treatment facilities in Richmond, Virginia and Charlotte, North Carolina.

JOURNAL PAGES

More titles of interest . . . .

From Anger to Forgiveness
by Earnie Larsen with Carol Larsen Hegarty

A practical guide to breaking the negative power of anger that can miscolor emotions and prevent us from reconciling conflicts. Unlike most anger books that help us label and express outrage, this book spells out the process of moving beyond expression to true healing. Earnie Larsen provides an understanding of how anger is still affecting the quality of our daily life. Here are lessons in empowerment through facing facts, digging out the roots of resentment, and creating a personal mind-set that makes forgiveness possible. 165 pp.
Order No. 5179

Of Course You're Angry, 2nd Edition
A Guide to Dealing with the Emotions of Chemical Dependence
by Gayle Rosellini and Mark Worden

Anger can be our worst enemy. Now we can discover how to cope positively with this natural emotion. This book explores the many masks of anger—violence, depression, and manipulation, and more—and explains how anger blocks self-understanding and growth. It gives us the tools to express anger in ways that lead to problem solving and forgiveness. 96 pp.
Order No. 1169

Touchstones
A Book of Daily Meditations for Men

This popular book opens us, as men, to a new awareness of our masculinity, home life, intimate relationships, values, children, and compassion. More than 150 topics in 366 daily meditations offer daily spiritual guidance grounded in the Twelve Steps to help us express feelings, reconnect with our souls and reclaim our deeper masculine qualities. A great source of topics for discussion groups. 400 pp.
Order No. 5029

The Promise of a New Day
A Book of Daily Meditations
by Karen Casey and Martha Vanceburg

Each day many women turn to these daily reflections for simple, inspiring wisdom about creating and maintaining inner peace. Here are reminders to give full attention to today, listen closely, understand that pain is inevitable but suffering is optional, and that there is something to learn from each experience. A book filled with hope. 400 pp.
Order No. 1045

For price and order information, or a free catalog, please
call our Telephone Representatives.

HAZELDEN

1-800-328-9000	1-651-213-4000	1-651-213-4590
(Toll Free, U.S., Canada, & the Virgin Islands)	(Outside the U.S. and Canada)	(24-Hour FAX) http://www.hazelden.org

Pleasant Valley Road • P.O. Box 176 • Center City, MN 55012-0176